Windows® 95
Made Simple

P.K.McBride

MADE SIMPLE
BOOKS

Made Simple
An imprint of Butterworth Heinemann
Linacre House, Jordan Hill, Oxford OX2 8DP
225 Wildwood Avenue, Woburn, MA 01801-2041
A division of Reed Educational and Professional Publishing Ltd

A member of the Reed Elsevier plc group

OXFORD   AUCKLAND   BOSTON
JOHANNESBURG   MELBOURNE   NEW DELHI

First published 1995
Reprinted 1996 (twice), 1997 (three times), 1998, 1999

TRADEMARKS/REGISTERED TRADEMARKS
Computer hardware and software brand names mentioned in this book are protected
by their respective trademarks and are acknowledged.

British Library Cataloguing in Publication Data
A catalogue record for this book is available from the British Library

ISBN 0 7506 23063

Typeset by P.K.McBride, Southampton

Archtype, Bash Casual, Cotswold and Gravity fonts from Advanced Graphics Ltd
Icons designed by Sarah Ward © 1994
Printed and bound in Great Britain by Scotprint, Musselburgh

Contents

Preface

Many of you who are using or are about to start using Windows 95 will have previously used Windows 3.1. You will find many similarities in this new system, but you will also find that quite a number of the old concepts and ways of working no longer hold true. A few of you will have been working with MS-DOS or even OS/2. For some – and an increasing number as time goes on – it will be your first experience of a computer operating system.

I have tried to write with all of you in mind, and that has not been as difficult as it may sound. I believe that the best way to approach Windows 95 is to forget anything you may know about Windows 3.1 and start from scratch. If you insist on hanging on to your Windows 3.1 baggage, it will just slow you down – you will keep trying to do things the old way, and get frustrated because some won't work. However, your hard-won Windows 3.1 experience will not be wasted, for when you do find things that are similar to what you were used to, you will pick them up very quickly.

And here's a reassuring thought for anyone still doubtful about switching. This book was written and typeset on a system running Windows 95. It has proved to be more reliable, easier to use and quicker than it was under Window 3.1.

1 Setting up

Before you start..

..ask yourself, 'Do I really want to do this?' If your system is working perfectly well under Windows 3.1, why should you change to Windows 95?

There are some very good reasons:

- Windows 3.1 is a fancy front-end that uses DOS to do the dirty work – Windows 95 is an integrated system. By cutting out DOS, programs run faster!

- Windows 3.1 used 16-bit for much of its data transfer – Windows 95 is fully 32-bit. Data moves faster!

- Windows 95 has broken through the old DOS 640k limit, so that all parts of the available memory can be accessed just as easily. Task switching is faster!

- The new Desktop gives quicker access to your most commonly used programs and easier switching between windows. You work faster!

- Windows 95 is truly multi-tasking, capable of printing or running a database query (or both) while you are working in another application. Jobs get done faster!

- Built-in network and communications support gives simple access to the Internet and to sending and receiving faxes and e-mail – with a suitable modem.

- The new Plug and Play approach to hardware will make it easier to add new kit to your system.

- Long filenames – breaching the old 8-character plus extension limit – identify files more clearly.

And why not?

- ❑ Some Windows 3.1 and DOS programs will not work with Windows 95 – one of your favourites might be amongst these.

- ❑ Despite the massive testing program, there may still be some bugs in the first edition.

- ❑ You may need a more powerful PC to run Windows 95

The platform

Theoretical minimum

> 386 processor
> 4 Mb RAM
> 100Mb hard drive
> Floppy disk

Practical minimum

> 486 processor
> 8 Mb RAM
> 300 Mb hard disk
> CD-ROM
> Sound card

Preparing for the worst

1 Either **backup** or **copy** the old DOS and Windows directories to a safe place.

2 Create a **System disk**.

3 Make WINDOWS and DOS directories on the floppy and copy in any essential files.

4 Copy onto it the AUTOEXEC.BAT and CONFIG.SYS files. Edit these so they run the programs on the floppy; e.g.

A:\DOS\SHARE.EXE /l:500

A:\WINDOWS\SMARTDRV.EXE

❑ **Recovery**

1 Restart from your system disk

2 Delete the WINDOWS and DOS directories

3 Copy the old ones back

4 Sell this book.

If your system may not be able to cope with Windows 95, or you use specialist software that may not be compatible, you must be able to reinstall Windows 3.1. Windows 95 prepares for this by making a compressed copy of the files from your DOS and WINDOWS directories, and providing an UNINSTALL utility. You should be able to run SETUP again and use this to remove Windows 95 and restore your old files. However, if you want to be on the safe side, it wouldn't hurt to make your own preparations.

To do this, you need a system disk with a full set of start-up files. Include copies of all the programs that are run from AUTOEXEC.BAT and CONFIG.SYS, so that you can do a proper start-up from the system disk. You should also **copy** (not move) your DOS, WINDOWS and WINDOWS/SYSTEM directories onto a second drive, if present, or into a new directory (perhaps called OLDSETUP). This would also be a good time to do a full backup onto a tape streamer, removable hard disk or set of floppies.

If Windows 95 doesn't do what you want, you can get back to Windows 3.1 without too much trouble.

The Setup Wizard

Setting up Windows 95 is largely a matter of responding to prompts as the Setup Wizard runs its course. However, there are a few points to watch out for.

- Allow at least an hour for installation – the Wizard may be able to do its stuff in 30 minutes, but you have to make some decisions, and that takes time.

- Accept all suggested settings, except for the few pointed out in the Steps

- There are three main Setup options – **Typical** is the right one for most people; **Compact** will save a few Mb of space; **Portable** adds utilities for transferring data to and from portable PCs.

- Installing all the **Components** takes around 75Mb of space; cutting out the Accessories, Networking and other optional extras reduces this to under 40Mb.

- Don't install the **Mail** unless you are on a network

- Do accept the offer of making a **Startup disk**. You may need it some day.

Basic steps

1 Close down all applications except File Manager.

2 Find and run the SETUP.EXE program on your installation disks or CD-ROM

3 Accept the defaults and keep clicking Next until you reach **Setup Options**. Do you want a *Typical*, *Compact* or *Portable* setup?

4 At the **Windows Components** panel it is simplest to go for the **most common** option. You can add and remove components later when Windows is running.

5 If you want to make your own selection now, see page 6.

6 When the Wizard reaches the file copying stage, go and make a cuppa. It won't need you for a while.

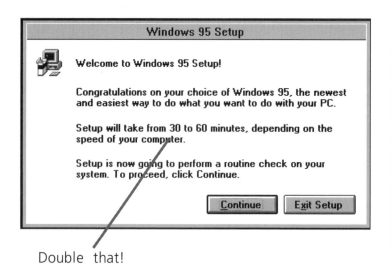

Double that!

4

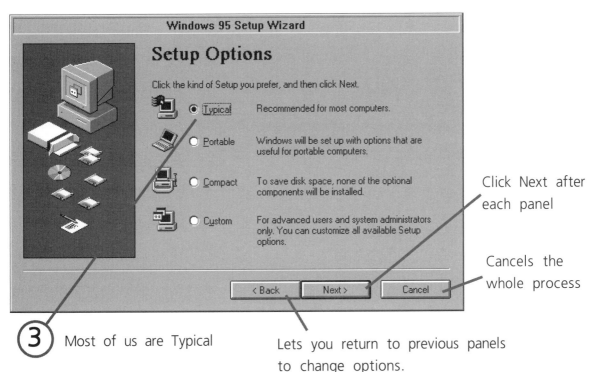

Click Next after each panel

Cancels the whole process

③ Most of us are Typical

Lets you return to previous panels to change options.

Tip

If the system seems to hang at times, don't panic. Every step takes longer than you think.

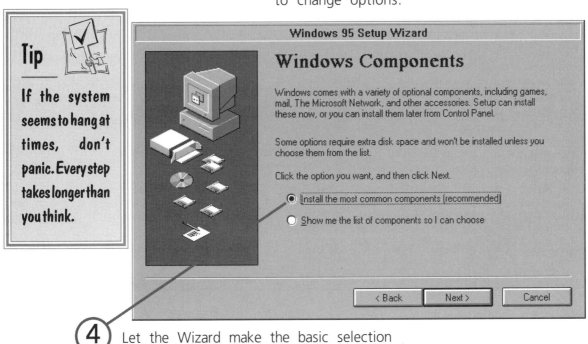

④ Let the Wizard make the basic selection

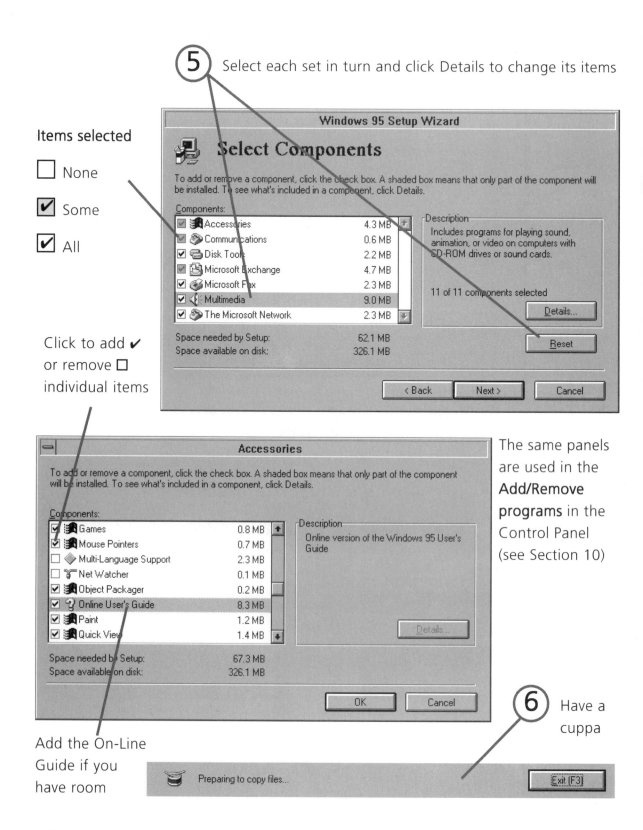

⑤ Select each set in turn and click Details to change its items

Items selected

☐ None

☑ Some

☑ All

Click to add ✔
or remove ☐
individual items

Windows 95 Setup Wizard

Select Components

To add or remove a component, click the check box. A shaded box means that only part of the component will be installed. To see what's included in a component, click Details.

Components:

☑ 📠 Accessories	4.3 MB	
☑ 📠 Communications	0.6 MB	
☑ 📠 Disk Tools	2.2 MB	
☑ 📠 Microsoft Exchange	4.7 MB	
☑ 📠 Microsoft Fax	2.3 MB	
☑ 📠 Multimedia	9.0 MB	
☑ 📠 The Microsoft Network	2.3 MB	

Description
Includes programs for playing sound, animation, or video on computers with CD-ROM drives or sound cards.

11 of 11 components selected

Details...

Space needed by Setup: 62.1 MB
Space available on disk: 326.1 MB

Reset

< Back   Next >   Cancel

Accessories

To add or remove a component, click the check box. A shaded box means that only part of the component will be installed. To see what's included in a component, click Details.

Components:

☑ 📠 Games	0.8 MB	
☑ 📠 Mouse Pointers	0.7 MB	
☐ ◈ Multi-Language Support	2.3 MB	
☐ 🔧 Net Watcher	0.1 MB	
☑ 📠 Object Packager	0.2 MB	
☑ ❓ Online User's Guide	8.3 MB	
☑ 📠 Paint	1.2 MB	
☑ 📠 Quick View	1.4 MB	

Description
Online version of the Windows 95 User's Guide

Details...

Space needed by Setup: 67.3 MB
Space available on disk: 326.1 MB

OK   Cancel

Add the On-Line
Guide if you
have room

The same panels
are used in the
**Add/Remove
programs** in the
Control Panel
(see Section 10)

⑥ Have a
cuppa

🎩 Preparing to copy files...

Exit (F3)

Taking the Tour

Tip

Check out What's New on the Welcome screen for a quick overview of the new features of Windows 95.

When the PC restarts, running Windows 95 for the first time, it will take a while to get going. Be patient – it's got a lot to think about. You will know you are there when you see the Welcome screen. If you have Windows 95 on CD, you will be offered the Tour. Take it! It only lasts a few minutes, but it will make you aware of some of the possibilities and features of the system.

Click this during the Tour to get back to the main menu

Exit at any point

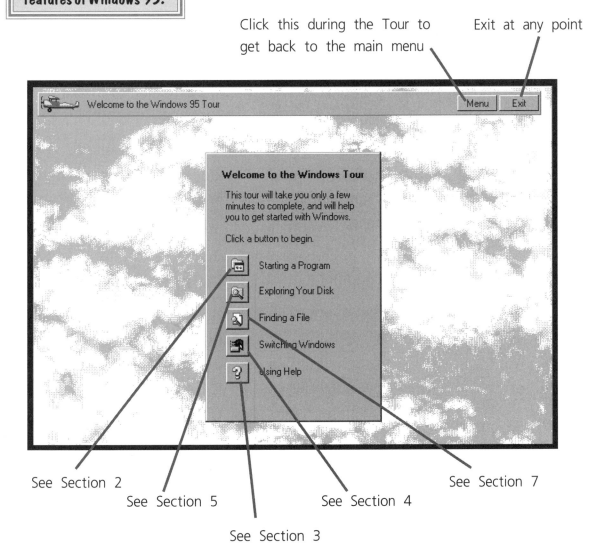

See Section 2

See Section 5

See Section 3

See Section 4

See Section 7

Summary

❏ Windows 95 is a more advanced system than Windows 3.1 but needs a **more powerful** PC.

❏ Most, but not all, **existing Windows and DOS software** will run under Windows 95.

❏ If the worst comes to the worst, you can **uninstall** Windows 95 and restore your old system.

❏ **Installation** is a slow process, but easy to do, thanks to the Wizard.

❏ You can use one of the predefined Setups or make your own selection of **components**.

❏ The **Tour** takes only a few moments, but gives a useful overview of Windows 95.

2 Start here

The Desktop

Windows is a Graphical User Interface (or **GUI**, pronounced *gooey*). What this means is that you work mainly by pointing at and clicking on symbols on the screen, rather than by typing commands. It is largely intuitive – i.e. the obvious thing to do is probably the right thing, and it is tolerant of mistakes. Many can be corrected as long as you tackle them straight away, and many others can be corrected easily, even after time has passed.

One of the ideas behind the design of Windows and of most Windows applications is that you should treat the screen as you would a desk. This is where you lay out your papers and books and tools to suit your own way of working. You may want to have more than one set of papers on the desktop at a time – so Windows lets you run several programs at once. You may want to have all your papers visible, for comparing or transferring data; you may want to concentrate on one, but have the others to hand. These – and other arrangements – are all possible.

Each program runs in its own window, and these can be arranged side by side, overlapping, or with the one you are working on filling the desktop and the others tucked out of the way, but still instantly accessible.

Just as there are many ways of arranging your desktop, so there are many ways of working with it – in fact, you are sometimes spoiled for choice!

It's your desktop. How you arrange it, and how you use it is up to you. This book will show you the simplest ways to use Windows 95 effectively.

❑ What you see on screen when you start Windows depends upon how the Desktop settings and shortcuts you are using.

❑ What the screen looks like once you are into your working session, is infinitely variable.

❑ Certain principles always apply and certain things are always there. It is the fact that all Windows applications share a common approach that makes Windows so easy to use.

Desktop – you can change the background pattern and the colours that are used.

Shortcuts – instant access to programs. You can create your own shortcuts.

Program windows – adjust their size and placing to suit yourself.

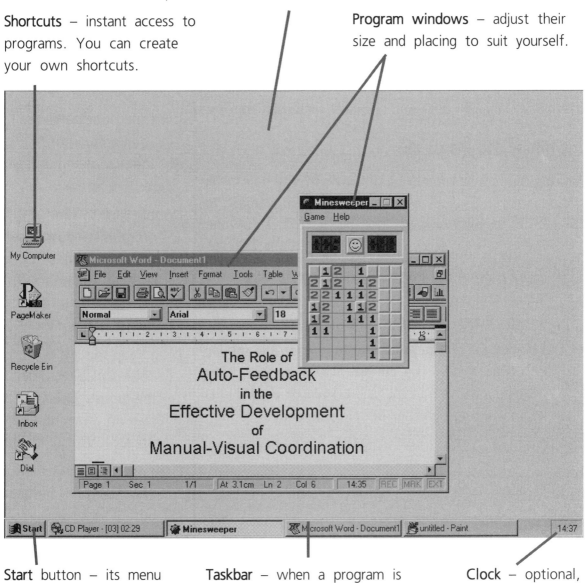

Start button – its menu holds all the applications and accessories on your system.

Taskbar – when a program is running, it has a button here. Click on a button to bring its program to the top.

Clock – optional, but handy

Taming the mouse

You can't do much in Windows until you have tamed the mouse. It is used for locating the cursor, for selecting from menus, highlighting, moving and changing the size of objects, and much more. It won't bite, but it will wriggle until you have shown it who's in charge.

To control the mouse effectively you need a mouse mat or a thin pad of paper – mice don't run well on hard desktops.

The mouse and the cursor

Moving the mouse rolls the ball inside it. The ball turns the sensor rollers and these transmit the movement to the cursor. Straightforward? Yes, but note these points.

● If you are so close to the edge of the mat that you cannot move the cursor any further, pick up the mouse and plonk it back into the middle. If the ball doesn't move, the cursor doesn't move.

● You can set up the mouse so that when the mouse is moved faster, the cursor moves further. (See *Adjusting the mouse*, page 116.) Watch out for this when working on other people's machines.

Tip

A clean mouse is a happy mouse. If it starts to play up, take out the ball and clean it and the rollers with a damp tissue. Check for fluff build-up on the roller axles and remove any with tweezers.

Mouse actions

Point Move the cursor with your fingers **off** the buttons.

Click the left button to select a file, menu item or other object.

Click the right button to open a menu of commands that apply to that object.

Double click to run programs. You can set the gap between clicks to suit yourself. (See *Adjusting the mouse*, page 116.)

Drag Keep the left button down while moving the mouse. Used for resizing, drawing and similar jobs.

Drag and drop Drag an object and release the button when it is in the right place. Used for moving objects.

Key guide

[Esc] – to Escape from trouble. Use it to cancel bad choices.

[Tab] – often used to move between objects on screen.

[Caps Lock] – only put this on when you want to type a lot of capitals. The **Caps Lock** light shows if it is on.

[Shift] – use it for capitals and the symbols on the number keys.

[Ctrl] – often used with other keys to give keystroke alternatives to mouse commands.

[Alt] – used, like [Ctrl], in combination with other keys.

[Backspace] - rubs out the character to the left of the text cursor.

[Enter] – used at the end of a piece of text or to start an operation.

[Delete] – deletes files, folders and screen objects. Use with care.

The keyboard

Most Windows 95 operations can be handled quite happily by the mouse alone, leaving the keyboard for data entry. However, keys are necessary for some jobs, and if you prefer typing to mousing, it is possible to do most jobs from the keyboard. The relevant ones are shown here.

The function keys

Many operations can be run from these – if you can be bothered to learn the keystrokes. The only one really worth remembering is [F1]. This will always call up Help.

The control sets

The **Arrow** keys can often be used instead of the mouse for moving the cursor. Above them are more movement keys, which will let you jump around in text. [Insert] and [Delete] are also here. (See the Key guide.)

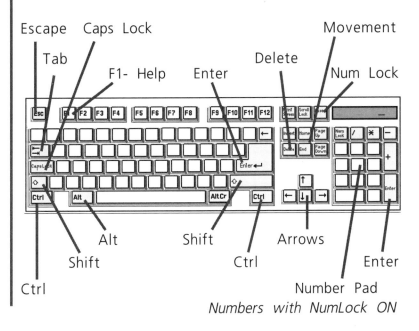

Numbers with NumLock ON

Making choices

There are many situations where you have to specify a filename or an option. Sometimes you have to type in what you want, but in most cases, it only takes a click of the mouse or a couple of keystrokes.

Menus

To pull one down from the menu bar click on it, or press [Alt] and the underlined letter – usually the initial.

To select an item from a menu, click on it or type its underlined letter.

Some items are *toggles*. Selecting them turns an option on or off. ✔ beside the name shows that the option is on.

▶ after an item shows that another menu leads from it.

If you select an item with three dots ... after it, a dialog box will open to get more information from you.

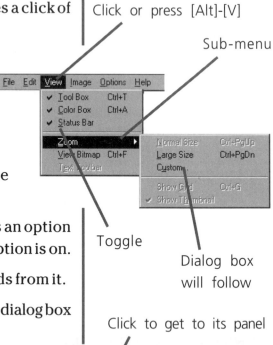

Click or press [Alt]-[V]

Sub-menu

Toggle

Dialog box will follow

Dialog boxes

These vary, but will usually have:

- | OK | to click when you have set the options, selected the file or whatever;

- | Apply | fix the options selected so far, but not leave the box;

- | Cancel | in case you decide the whole thing was a mistake;

- | Help | or 🔧 to get help on items in the box.

Click to get to its panel

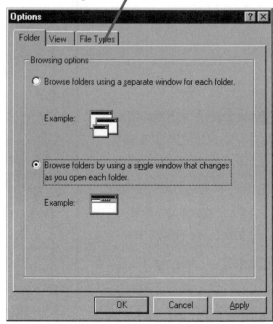

Tabs and panels

Some dialog boxes have several sets of options in them, each on a separate panel. These are identified by tabs at the top. Click on a tab to bring its panel to the front. Usually clicking [OK] on any panel will close the whole box. Use [Apply] when you have finished with one panel but want to explore others before closing.

Check boxes

These are used where there are several options, and you can use as many as you like at the same time.

✔ in the box shows that the option has been selected.

If the box is grey and the caption faint, the option is not available for the selected item.

Only this one

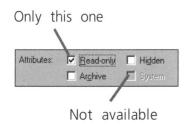

Not available

Radio buttons

These are used for either-or options. Only one of the set can be selected.

The selected option is shown by black blob in the middle.

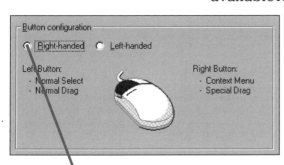

This one please

Drop-down lists

Click here...

If a slot has a down arrow button on its right, click the button to drop down a list.

Click on an item in the list to select.

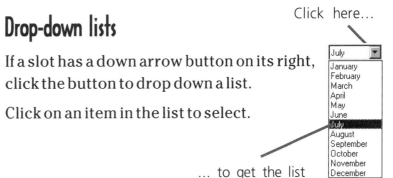

... to get the list

15

Welcome!

When Windows 95 starts up, it first displays a friendly welcome. The **Did you know...** tip is different every time and can be very useful, but after a few sessions you may feel that you have been welcomed enough. When you reach that point, you can stop it from reappearing.

Take the tour (page 7) – needs the installation CD-ROM

See the main changes from Windows 3.1

Read the adverts – needs the installation CD-ROM

Display another tip

Go to work

Click to close

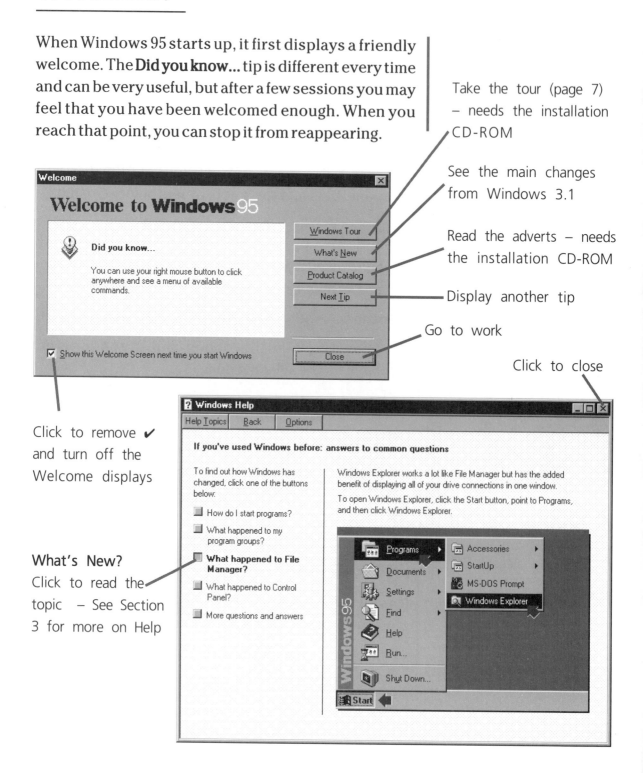

Click to remove ✔ and turn off the Welcome displays

What's New?
Click to read the topic – See Section 3 for more on Help

The Start menu

Clicking on 🏁Start at the bottom left of the screen, takes you into the menu system from which you can run applications, get help, find files, customize your system and close down at the end of a session.

The first level menu has 7 options:

Programs is the main route to your applications. It is the equivalent of Program Manager in Windows 3.1. Leading from this is a second level of program folders, and selecting from there takes you to the icons for the programs in each folder.

Documents holds a list of recently used document files. Selecting one from this list will run the relevant application and open the file for you to work on.

Settings is used to customize the desktop and other aspects of the system (Section 10), set up printers (Section 11) and even rewrite the menu (Section 9)

Find will track down files and folders on your computer – and on your local network or the Microsoft Network if you are connected.

Help is one way into the Help system (Section 3)

Run lets you run a named application or starts up work on a document. You would mainly use this for installing new software or for handling a file that you have brought in on a floppy disk.

Shut down is the only safe way to end a session.

Running a program

If you know where a program is in the menu structure, running it should take no more than a few mouse moves and clicks. Even if you do not know where it is, it will take only a few moments longer to browse through the menus to find and run it.

1 Click **Start**

2 Point to **Programs**. The program folder menu opens.

3 Point to the folder that contains the program – if you cannot see it in that menu, point to another item and check its menu.

❏ You may have to repeat Step 3 as some folders have other folders within them.

4 Click once on the program to run it.

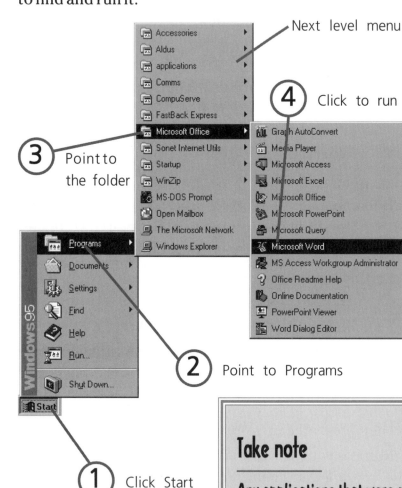

Next level menu

④ Click to run

③ Point to the folder

② Point to Programs

① Click Start

Take note

Any applications that were on your PC before you installed Windows 95 should have been brought into the Start menu; any that came in with Windows 95 will be there; any that you install later should slot themselves into the menus, and you can add others at any time.

18

Basic steps

1 Click 🔳 Start

2 Point to **Documents**

3 Click on the file to get started on it.

Icons and extensions

 AVI – multimedia

 BMP – Bitmap graphic

 DOC – Word for Windows

 TTF – True Type Font

 TXT – Plain text file

 XLS – Excel spreadsheet

 ZIP – WinZip compressed file

Working from documents

The Documents item on the Start menu brings up a list of files that you have recently used. Selecting one of these will start the relevant application and load in the document.

There is room for 15 documents in the list. Once you hit the limit, new documents push out the oldest ones.

Each document is accompanied by a little icon, to help identify the type of file. There must be hundreds of different icons, but you will soon come to recognise those of types that you use regularly. A few of the more common ones are listed on the right.

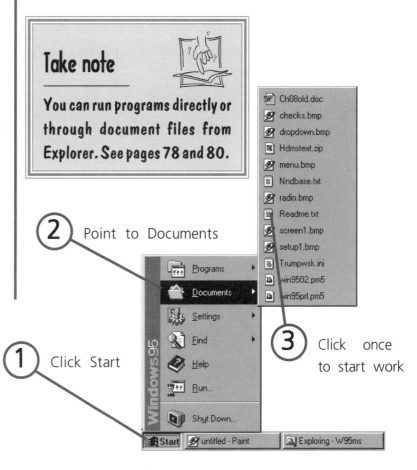

Take note

You can run programs directly or through document files from Explorer. See pages 78 and 80.

② Point to Documents

① Click Start

③ Click once to start work

Short menus

If you click the right button on almost anything on screen in Windows 95, a short menu will open beside it. This contains a set of commands and options that can be applied to the object.

What is on the menu depends upon the type of object. Three are shown here to give an idea of the possibilities.

Properties

Most menus have a **Properties** item. The contents of its dialog box also vary according to the nature of the object. For shortcuts, like the one for the Phone Dialer shown below, there is a *Shortcut* panel that controls the link to the program. The (hidden) *General* panel has a description of the file – this panel is in every file's Properties box.

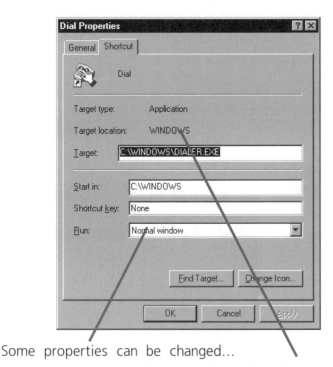

Some properties can be changed...

...others are there for information only

Files can be Opened, Sent to a removable disk or off in the mail, and Deleted – amongst other things.

The **Clock** can be adjusted, and as it is on the Taskbar, you can also arrange the screen display from this menu.

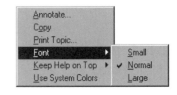

Help pages can be Annotated or Printed – you can even adjust the Font size.

Basic steps

1 Click 🔳 Start

2 Click **Shut down**

3 If you want to restart, set the option.

4 Click **Yes**

Tip

If you want to run an MS-DOS application, you can do so from the MS-DOS Prompt on the Programs menu, rather than by exiting to MS-DOS mode. Working from within the Prompt, you can task switch and transfer data between DOS and Windows applications. (See the MS_DOS Prompt, page 142.)

Shutting down

When you have finished work on your computer, you must shut it down properly, and not just turn it off. This is essential. During your work session, applications and Windows 95 may have created temporary work files – including the swap file which can get very large if you run several applications at once, and data files that you have been editing may still be open in a memory buffer and not yet written safely to disk. An organised shut down closes and stores open files and clears away unwanted ones.

Sometimes you will find that a bug in an application or in Windows 95 has made the system hang or otherwise misbehave. Press **[Ctrl]-[Alt]-[Delete]** together to close that application, then shut down and restart. That generally clears most problems.

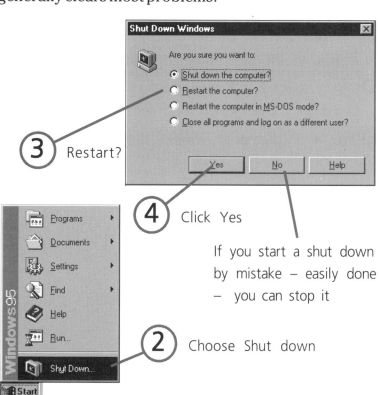

③ Restart?

④ Click Yes

If you start a shut down by mistake – easily done – you can stop it

① Click Start

② Choose Shut down

Summary

❑ Windows is an **intuitive** system – if something *feels* right, it probably *is* right.

❑ All Windows software works in much the same way, so once you have got the hang on one program, you are half way to learning the next.

❑ The **mouse** is an important tool. Practice using it – a good excuse for playing the games!

❑ Some operations are easier with **keys**, and just a few can only be done from the keyboard.

❑ **Selections** can usually be made by picking from a list or clicking on a button or check box.

❑ The **Start** button is the main way into the system. Get to know your way around its menus.

❑ Applications can be run directly from the **Programs** menu, or through files in the **Documents** list.

❑ Every object has a **short menu** of common commands that can be used with it.

❑ You must **shut down** properly at the end of a session.

3 Help!

Help topics

You can get help in several different ways:

- The main Help topics, run from the Start menu;
- Help topics on applications and accessories, run from their menus;
- Query help on dialog boxes;

In all Help topics systems there are three approaches:

- an organised **Contents** list;
- **Index**ed Help pages;
- a word-based **Find** facility.

❑ **From the Desktop**

1 Click

2 Click on **Help**

❑ **From an application**

1 Click on **Help** on the menu bar

2 Select **Help Topics**

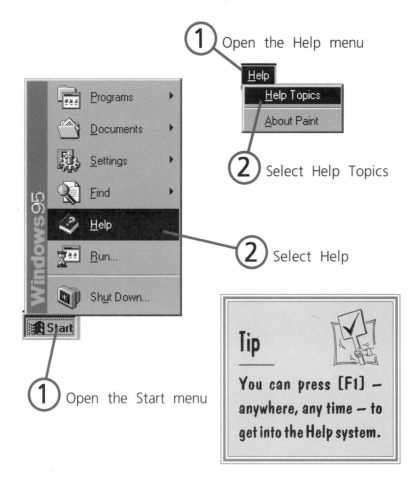

① Open the Help menu

② Select Help Topics

② Select Help

① Open the Start menu

Take note

Windows 3.1 applications have a slightly different Help menu. In these, select Help – Contents to get to the topics pages. The Index and Find facilities are reached through Help – Search.

Tip

You can press [F1] – anywhere, any time – to get into the Help system.

Basic steps

1 Click the **Contents** tab if this panel is not at the front already.

2 Point to 📖 and click [Display] to see the page titles.

3 Point to ⍰ and click [Display] to read the page.

either

4 Click **Help Topics** to return to the Contents panel

or

5 Click ☒ to close the page and exit Help

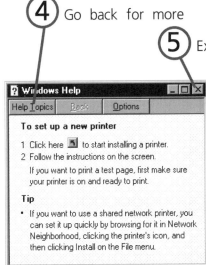

Contents

This approach treats the Help pages as a book. You scan through the headings to find a section that seems to cover what you want, and open that to see the page titles. (Some sections have sub-sections, making it a 2 or 3 stage process to get to page titles.)

Some Help topics are stand alone pages; others have **Related topics** buttons to take you on to further pages.

② Open a book   ① Use the Contents panel

③ Open a page

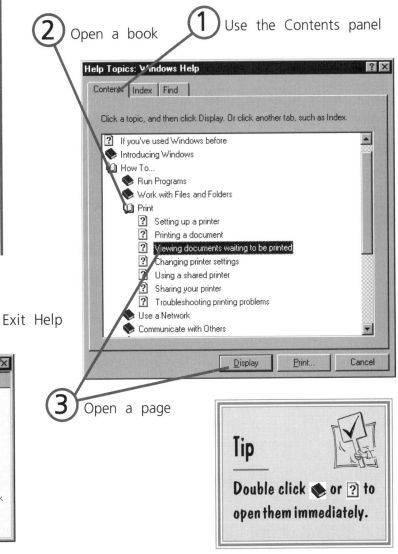

④ Go back for more

⑤ Exit Help

Tip

Double click 📖 or ⍰ to open them immediately.

25

Using the Index

Basic steps

1 Click the **Index** tab

2 Start to type a word into the slot to focus the entry list or use the scroll bar to find the topic.

3 Select the entry

4 Click [Display]

Though the Contents are good for getting an overview of how things work, if you want help on a specific problem – usually the case – you are better off with the Index.

This is organised through an cross-referenced list of terms. The main list is alphabetical, with sub-entries, just like the index in a book. And, as with an index in a book, you can plough through it slowly from the top, or skip through to find the words that start with the right letters. Once you find a suitable entry, you can display the list of cross-referenced topics and pick one of those.

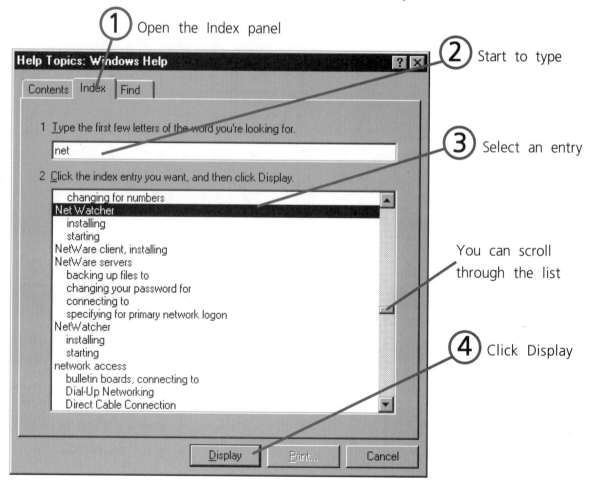

① Open the Index panel

② Start to type

③ Select an entry

You can scroll through the list

④ Click Display

5 Pick the most suitable topic from the Topics Found list

6 Click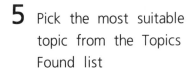

❏ The help page will open. When you have done with it you can click **Help Topics** to return to the Index or to close the page and exit Help

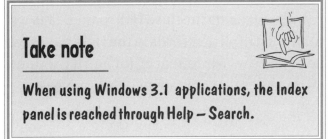

Take note

When using Windows 3.1 applications, the Index panel is reached through Help – Search.

If you cannot see anything useful, close the panel and return to the Index

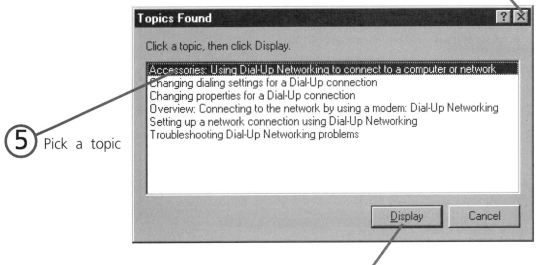

Topics Found

Click a topic, then click Display.

> Accessories: Using Dial-Up Networking to connect to a computer or network
> Changing dialing settings for a Dial-Up connection
> Changing properties for a Dial-Up connection
> Overview: Connecting to the network by using a modem: Dial-Up Networking
> Setting up a network connection using Dial-Up Networking
> Troubleshooting Dial-Up Networking problems

Display   Cancel

⑤ Pick a topic

⑥ Click Display

Take note

If there is only one relevant topic page, the system will bypass the Topics Found panel, and take you directly to the page after Step 4.

Finding help

If you can't track down the help you need from the Index, you can **Find** it using the third Help panel. This works by creating a list of all the words in the Help pages; you give it one or more words to search for and it produces a list of all the topics that contain matching words.

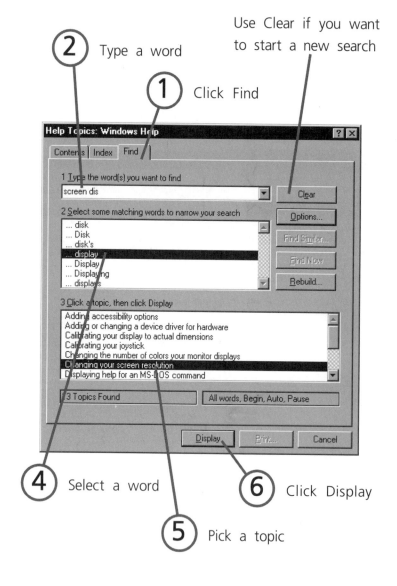

② Type a word

Use Clear if you want to start a new search

① Click Find

④ Select a word

⑥ Click Display

⑤ Pick a topic

Basic steps

1 Open the **Find** panel in **Help Topics**

2 Type your word into the top slot. As you type, words starting with the typed letters appear in the pane beneath.

3 If you want to narrow the search, go back to step 2, type a space after your first word and give another.

4 Select the most suitable word from the **Narrow the search** pane

5 Select a topic from the lower pane

6 Click ⬚ Display ⬚

Tip

If you want to have the Help page in sight, right click on it, to open its short menu and set **Keep Help on Top** to **On**.

Basic steps

❑ **Narrowing the scope**

1 On the **Find** panel, click [Options...] .

2 On the **Find Options** panel, click [Files...]

❑ This shows a list of the Help files that will be searched. Some of these are not relevant.

3 Hold **[Ctrl]** and click on the files that you want it to ignore. If you remove one by mistake, click again to reselect it.

4 Click [OK] then close the **Options** panel.

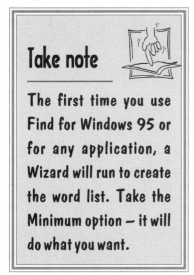

Take note

The first time you use Find for Windows 95 or for any application, a Wizard will run to create the word list. Take the Minimum option – it will do what you want.

Find options

There are several Options that you can set to alter the nature of the search or narrow its scope.

In the **Search for words containing** box, select

All the words.. where you are using several words to focus on one topic

At least one.. where you are giving several alternatives in the hope that it recognises one

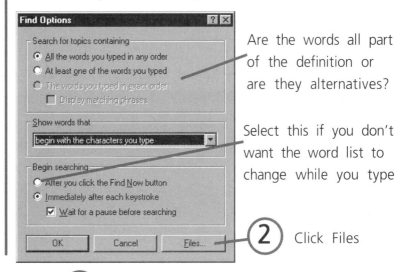

Are the words all part of the definition or are they alternatives?

Select this if you don't want the word list to change while you type

(2) Click Files

(3) [Ctrl] and click to remove or reselect

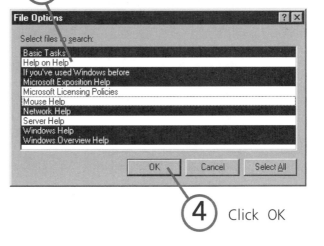

(4) Click OK

Instant help

As well as the main Help system, Windows 95 offers a couple of other brief, but useful, forms of help.

The query icon

All dialog boxes and panels in Windows 95 and its components – and in newer applications – have an 🔲 icon on the top right of the status bar. You will also find an ⬛ icon on the toolbar of some applications. They can both be used for finding out more about objects on screen.

Basic steps

1 Click on the 🔲 or ⬛ icon.

2 Click the ⬛ cursor on the button, option or other item that you want to know about.

3 After you have read the help box, click anywhere to close it.

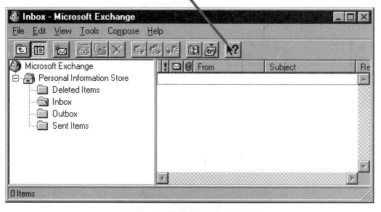

Click the query icon

Take note

You only get one help box for each click on the query icon, though you can use that as often as you like.

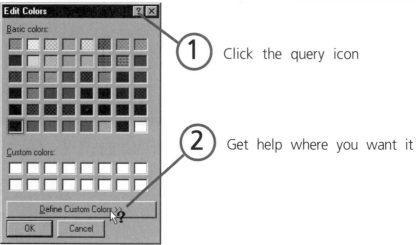

① Click the query icon

② Get help where you want it

30

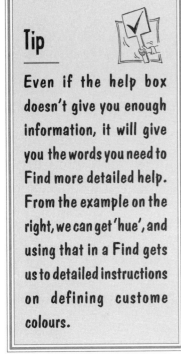
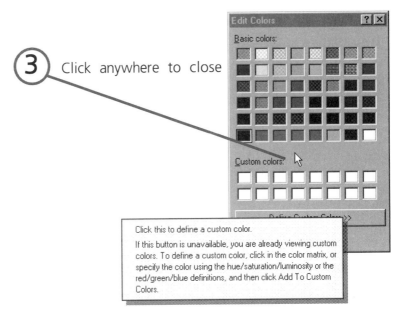

③ Click anywhere to close

Click this to define a custom color.

If this button is unavailable, you are already viewing custom colors. To define a custom color, click in the color matrix, or specify the color using the hue/saturation/luminosity or the red/green/blue definitions, and then click Add To Custom Colors.

Help on icons

Icons are supposed to be self-explanatory, but their purpose can not always be summed up in a small image. Never fear, help is near!

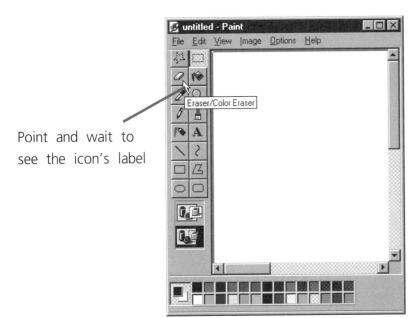

Point and wait to see the icon's label

Let the cursor rest over an icon for a moment and a label will pop up to tell you what it is. If that isn't enough to tell you what it does, at least you have a name to look up in the Help Index.

Summary

❑ Help is always available.

❑ Use the **Contents** panel when you are browsing to see what topics are covered.

❑ Use the **Index** to go directly to the help on a specified operation or object.

❑ If you can't locate the help in the Index, use the **Find** facility to track down the pages.

❑ In Windows 3.1 applications, Find is called **Search**.

❑ For help with items in a **dialog box** or **panel**, click the query icon and point to the item.

❑ If you hold the cursor over an **icon**, a brief prompt will pop up to tell you what it does.

4 Window control

The window frame

This is more than just a pretty border. It contains all the controls you need for adjusting the display.

Frame edge

This has a control system built into it. When a window is in Restore mode – i.e. smaller than full-screen – you can drag on the edge to make it larger or smaller. (See *Changing the size*, page 41.)

Title bar

This is to remind you of where you are and is used for moving the window. Drag on this and the window moves. (See *Moving windows*, page 40.)

Maximize, Minimize and Restore

These buttons change the display mode. Only one of Maximize and Restore will be visible at any one time. (See *Window modes*, page 36.)

Close

One of several ways to close a window and the program that was running in it. (See *Closing windows*, page 43)

Control menu icon

There is no set image for this icon, as every application has its own, but clicking on whatever is here will open the Control menu. This can be used for changing the screen mode or closing the window. (See *Window modes*, page 36.) Double-clicking this icon will close down the window.

Take note

Most applications can handle several documents at once, each in its own window. These are used in almost the same way as program windows. The applications usually have a **Window** menu containing controls for the document windows.

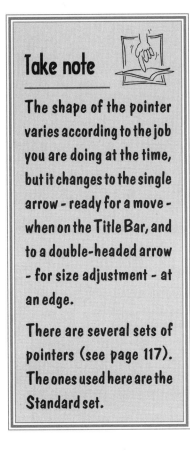
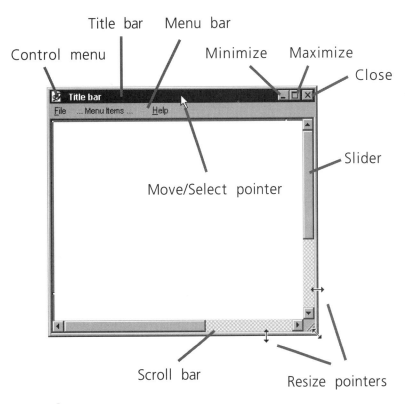

Control menu — Title bar — Menu bar — Minimize — Maximize — Close

Move/Select pointer

Slider

Scroll bar

Resize pointers

Menu bar

Immediately below the Title bar in an application's window is a bar containing the names of its menus. Clicking on one of these will drop down a list of commands.

Scroll bars

These are present on the right side and bottom of the frame if the display contained by the window is too big to fit within it. The **Sliders** in the Scroll Bars show you where your view is, relative to the overall display. Moving these allows you to view a different part of the display. (See *Scrolling*, page 42.)

Window modes

All programs are displayed on screen in windows, and these can normally have three modes:

- Maximized – filling the whole screen;
- Minimized – not displayed, though still present as a button on the Task bar;
- Restore – adjustable in size and in position.

Take note

Some applications run in small, fixed size windows, so Maximize and Restore do not apply to them.

Maximized

In Restore mode

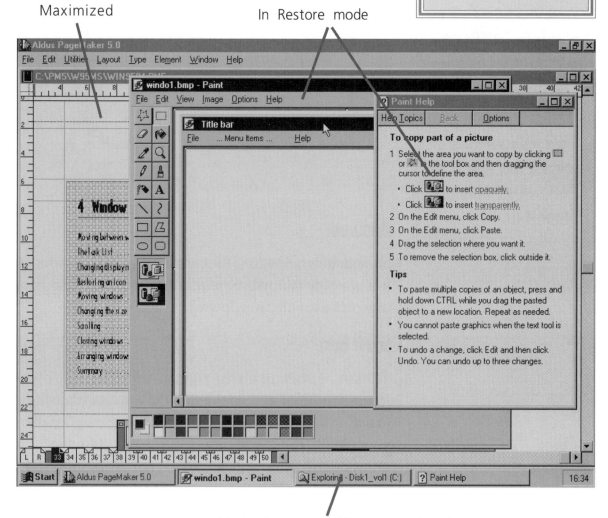

Minimized – not visible except for this

Basic steps

❏ To make a window full-screen

Click ▫ or select **Maximize** from the Control Menu

❏ To restore a window to variable size

Click ▫ or select **Restore** from the Control Menu

❏ To shrink a window to an icon

Click ▫ or select **Minimize** from the Control Menu

Changing display modes

Clicking on the buttons in the top right corner of the frame is the simplest way to switch between **Maximize** and **Restore** modes, and to **Minimize** a window. If you prefer it can be done using the Control Menu.

The Control menu

Click the icon at the top left to open this. Options that they don't apply at the time will be 'greyed out'. The menu here came from a variable size window. One from a full-screen window would have **Move**, **Size** and **Maximize** in grey.

Using the Taskbar

Click a program's button to bring its window to the top.

Right click the button to open the Control menu.

Left click to activate

Right click for the menu

Keyboard Control

[Alt]–[Space] opens the Control menu of an application.

[Alt]–[-] (minus) opens the Control menu of a document.

Minimized documents

When you minimize a document window, within an application, it shrinks to a tiny title bar, with just enough room for an abbreviated name and the icons. Click Maximize or Restore to open it out again.

Restore   Maximize

Arranging windows

If you want to have two or more windows visible at the same time, you will have to arrange them on your desktop. There are Windows tools that will do it for you, or you can do it yourself.

If you right click the Taskbar, its menu has options to arrange the windows on the desktop. Open it and you will see **Cascade**, **Tile Vertical** and **Tile Horizontal**. Similar options are on the Window menu of most applications, though these only affect the layout *within* the programs.

Cascade places the windows overlapping with just the title bars of the back ones showing. You might just as well Maximize the current window, and use the Taskbar buttons to get to the rest.

Either of the Tile layouts can be the basis of a well-arranged desktop.

1 Maximize or Restore the windows that you want to include in the layout. Minimize those that you will not be using actively.

2 Right click the Taskbar to open its menu

3 Select Tile Horizontal or Tile Vertical

4 If you only want to work in one window at a time, Maximize it, and Restore it back into the arrangement when you have done.

Tip

If you want to adjust the balance of the layout, you can move and resize the windows.

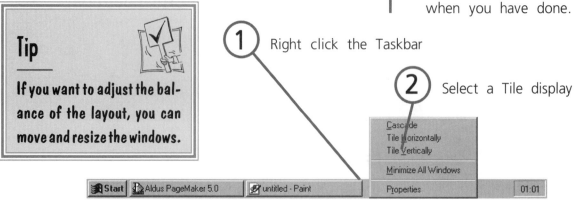

① Right click the Taskbar

② Select a Tile display

Tip

It is generally simplest to work with the active window Maximized and any others Minimized out of the way.

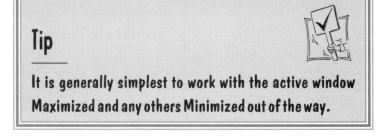

Tile

Tile displays are useful when copying between disks, as the limited view within each window does not make much difference

Tile arranges open windows side by side (Vertical), or in rows (Horizontal) – with more than three windows, the tiling is in both directions. As the window frames take up space, the actual working area is significantly reduced. You cannot do much serious typing in a tiled window.

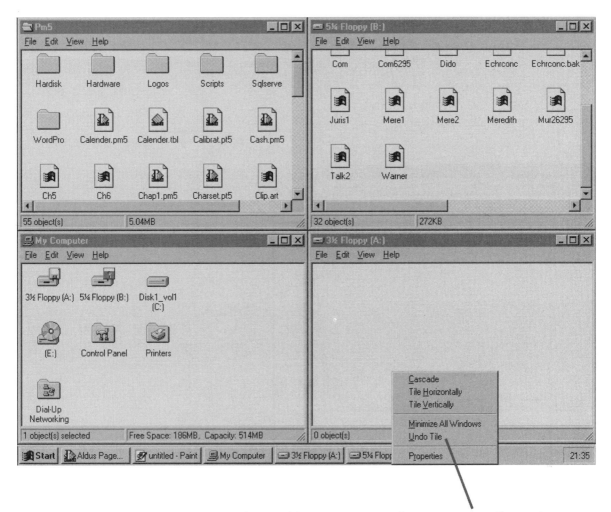

The Taskbar menu now has an Undo Tile option to restore your screen to its previous state.

Moving windows

When a window is in **Restore** mode – open but not full screen – it can be moved anywhere on the screen.

● If you are not careful it can be moved almost off the screen! Fortunately, at least a bit of the title bar will still be visible, and that is the handle you need to grab to pull it back into view.

Basic steps

1 If the Title Bar isn't highlighted, click on the window to make it the active one.

2 Point at the Title Bar and hold the left button down.

3 Drag the window to its new position – you will only see a grey outline moving.

4 Release the button.

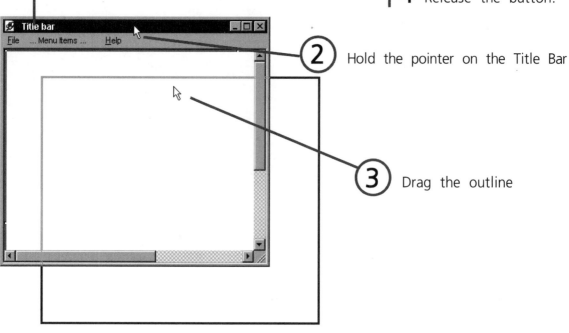

① Make the Window active

② Hold the pointer on the Title Bar

③ Drag the outline

④ Release to drop into its new position

40

Basic steps

1 Move the pointer to the edge or corner that you want to pull in or out.

2 When you see the double-headed arrow, hold down the left mouse button and drag the outline to the required size

3 Release the button.

Changing the size

When a window is in Restore mode, you can change its size and shape by dragging the edges of the frame to new positions.

Combined with the moving facility, this lets you arrange your desktop exactly the way you like it.

● The resize pointers only appear when the pointer is just on an edge, and they disapear again if you go too far. Practice! You'll soon get the knack of catching them.

You can drag any edge or corner

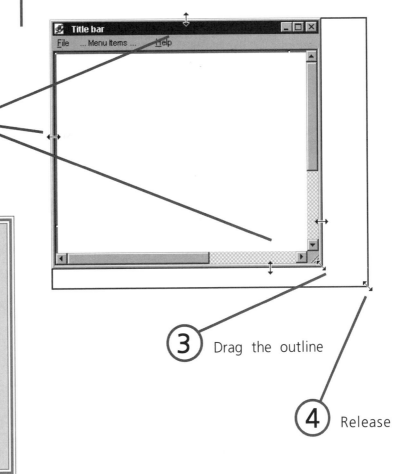

3 Drag the outline

4 Release

Tip

The quickest way your get a window the right size, in the right place, is to use the bottom right size handle to set the shape, then drag the window into position.

41

Scrolling

What you can see in a window is often only part of the story. The working area of the application may well be much larger. If there are scroll bars on the side and/or bottom of the window, this tells you that there is more material outside the frame. The scroll bars let you pull some of this material into view.

Tip

If a window is blank — and you think there should be something there — push the sliders to the very top and left. That's where your work is likely to be.

- ❏ Drag the **Slider** ▪ to scroll the view in the window. Keep your pointer moving straight along the bar or it won't work!

- ❏ Click an **Arrow** ▲ to edge the slider towards the arrow. Hold down for a slow continuous scroll.

- ❏ Click on the **Bar** be-side the Slider to make it jump towards the pointer.

Sliders

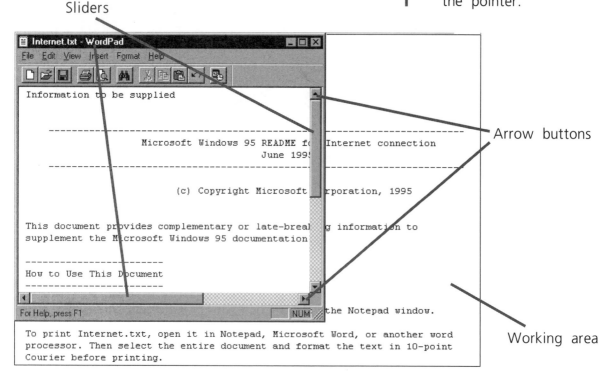

Arrow buttons

Working area

42

Basic steps

❑ **Closing an active window**

1 Click ⊠

or

1 Press [Alt]-[F4]

❑ **Closing from the Taskbar**

1 Right click the progam's button to get its menu

2 Select **Close**

3 If you have forgotten to save your work, take the opportunity that is offered to you.

Tip

When you have finished with a program, close it. Even Minimized windows use a little memory and slow down performance.

Closing windows

When you close a window, you close down the program that was running inside it.

If you haven't saved your work, most programs will point this out and give you a chance to save before closing.

There are at least 5 different ways of closing. Here are the simplest three:

● If the window is in Maximized or Restore mode, click the close icon at the top right of the Title bar. (If your mouse control is not too good, you may well do this when you are trying to Maximize the window!)

● If the window has been Minimized onto the Taskbar, right click on its button to open the Control menu and use **Close**.

● If you prefer working from keys, press **[Alt]-[F4]**.

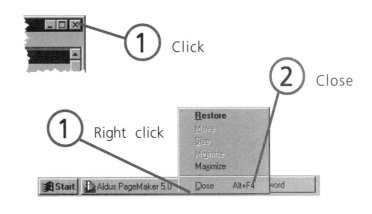

① Click

② Close

① Right click

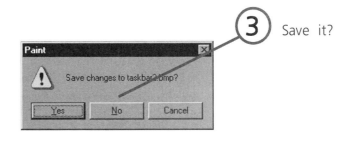

③ Save it?

43

Summary

❑ You can move between windows by clicking on any visible part of them – though the active parts of the frame should be avoided.

❑ Windows can be displayed in **Maximized** (full-screen) or **Restore** (variable size) modes, or **Minimized** to icons.

❑ **Minimized windows** can be restored to full size by clicking on them.

❑ Windows can be arranged on the desktop by picking **Cascade** or **Tile** from the **Task List** options.

❑ A window can be **moved** about the screen by dragging on its title bar.

❑ You can change the **size** by dragging on any of its edges.

❑ The **scroll bars** will let you move the working area inside a window.

❑ **Closing** a window closes its program.

44

5 Exploring folders

Explorer v. My Computer

Explorer, My Computer and Network Neighborhood are you main file and folder management tools.

Explorer

This is closely related to File Manager of Windows 3.1. It gives a dual display, with the folder structure on the left and the contents of the current folder on the right.

Though Explorer will only display the contents of one folder – there is no multi-window display as in File Manager – you can run two or more copies of it at once. This can be useful when you are moving or copying files from one part of the system to another.

Explorer can access the folders in all of the drives attached to your computer, and to any that may be accessible to you over a network.

My Computer

This has a simpler display than Explorer. It works in a single-pane window, and when first opened it gives an overview of the components of your own system. You can then open another window to get a detailed look at folders in a drive, and continue opening further windows to go deeper into folders.

Though Explorer gives a clearer view than My Computer of how your storage is organised, My Computer probably gives you a clearer view of any one part of the system.

Network Neighborhood

This is the same as My Computer, but opens with the focus on any networked machines.

Files and folders

❑ **Root** – the folder of the disk. All other folders branch off from the root.

❑ **Parent** – a folder that contains another.

❑ **Child** – a sub-folder of a Parent.

❑ **Branch** – the structure of sub-folders open off from a folder.

If you are going to work successfully with Windows 95 – or any computer system – you must understand how its disk storage is organised, and how to manage files efficiently and safely. In this section, we will look at the filing system, working with folders and the screen displays of Explorer and My Computer. In later sections, we will cover managing files and looking after your disks.

Folders

The hard disks supplied on modern PCs are typically 540 Megabytes or larger. A Megabyte is 1 million bytes and each byte can hold one character (or part of a number or graphic). That means that a typical hard disk can hold up to 80 million words – enough for 400 hefty novels! More to the point, if you were using it to store letters and reports, it could hold many thousands of files. It must be organised if you are ever to find your files.

Folders provide this organisation. They are containers in which related files can be placed to keep them together, and away from other files. A folder can also contain sub-folders – which can themselves by sub-divided. You can think of the first level of folders as being sets of filing cabinets; the second level are drawers within the cabinets, and the next level folders within the drawers. (And the folders could have sub-dividers – there is no limit to this.)

Tip

When planning the folder structure, keep it simple. Too many folders within folders can make it hard to find files.

Paths

The structure of folders is often referred to as the **tree**. It starts at the **root**, which is the drive letter – C: for your main hard disk – and branches off from there.

A folder's position in the tree is described by its **path**. For most operations, you can identify a folder by clicking on it in a screen display, but now and then you will have to type its path. This should start at the drive letter and the root, and include every folder along the branch, with a backslash (\) between the names.

For example:

C:\DTP

C:\WORDPROC\LETTERS

When you want to know a path, look it up in the Explorer display and trace the branches down from the root.

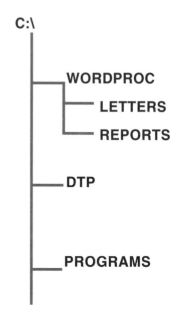

```
C:\
        WORDPROC
            LETTERS
            REPORTS
    DTP
    PROGRAMS
```

Filenames

A filename has two parts – the name and an extension.

The **name** is no longer restricted to 8 characters, as it was in DOS and Windows 3.1. It can be as long as you like, and include any characters – including spaces. But don't let the freedom go to your head. The longer the name, the greater the opportunity for typing errors. The most important thing to remember when giving a filename is that it must mean something to you, so that you can find it easily next time you come back to the job.

The **extension** can be from 0 to 3 characters, and is separated from the rest of the name by a dot. It is used to identify the nature of the file. Windows and MSDOS use the extensions COM, EXE, SYS, INI, DLL to identify special files of their own.

Take note

Whatever you call a file, Windows 95 will also give it a name in the 8.3 MSDOS format, for use with older applications. The MSDOS name will start with the same six letters, then have ~ and a number. 'LETTER TO BILL.DOC' will become 'LETTER~1.DOC'

48

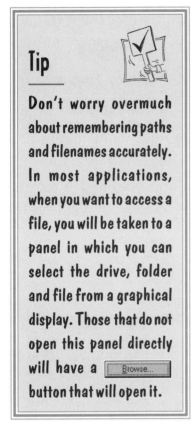
Most applications also use their own special extensions. Word-processor files are often marked with DOC or TXT; spreadsheet files are usually WQ1 or WK1; databases files typically have DB extensions.

If you are saving a file in a word-processor, spreadsheet or other application, and are asked for a filename, you normally only have to give the first part. The application will take care of the extension. If you do need to give an extension, make it meaningful. BAK is a good extension for backup files; TXT for text files.

When an application asks you for a filename – and the file is in the *current* folder – type in the name and extension only. If the file is in *another* folder, type in the path, a backslash separator and then the filename.

For example:

MYFILE.DOC

C:\WORPROC\REPORTS\MAY25.TXT

A:\MYFILE.BAK

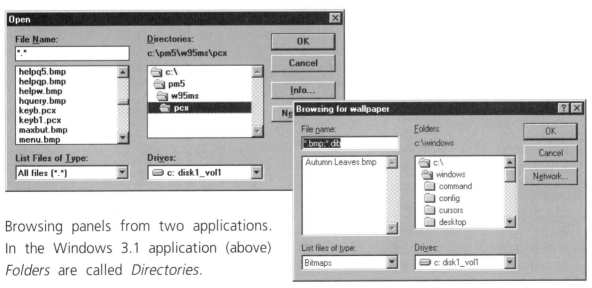

Browsing panels from two applications. In the Windows 3.1 application (above) *Folders* are called *Directories*.

The Explorer display

Explorer window has the usual frame controls and menu bar. The main working area is split, with the *All Folders* structure, or Tree, on the left, and the file list, or *Contents*, on the right.

The **All Folders** may show the disk drives and first level of folders only, but folders can be expanded to show some or all of the sub-folders. (See *Expanding folders*, overleaf.)

The **Contents** shows the files and sub-folders in the currently selected folder. These can be displayed as large or small icons accompanied by the name only, or with details of the file's size, type and date it was last modified. (See *Arranging icons*, page 62.)

The **Status line** shows the number of files in the folder, on the right, and the size of the selected files, on the left.

Basic steps

☐ Starting Explorer

1 Click 🏁 Start

2 Point to **Programs**

3 Click **Explorer**

4 Click on a folder's icon 📁 or its name to open 📂 it and display its Contents

Take note

The My Computer display is the same as that of Explorer, but without the All Folders pane. Its menu commands and Toolbar icons are identical.

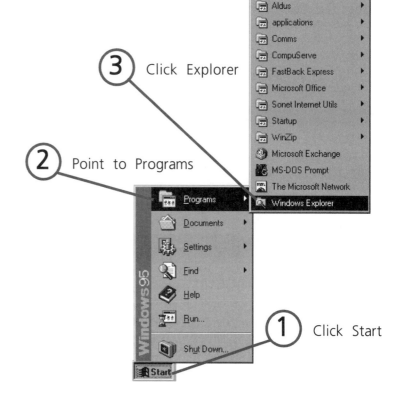

③ Click Explorer

② Point to Programs

① Click Start

50

Basic steps

- ❏ **Adding the Toolbar**
- **1** Open the **View** menu
- **2** Click beside **Toolbar** to give it a tick.

- ❏ **Icons and lists**
- **1** Open the **View** menu
- **2** Choose a display style.
- *or*
- **1** Click the Toolbar icon

Take note

The Toolbar icons are described on page 58.

View options

The View menu has several useful display options.

- ● If you prefer to work with icons, rather than menu commands, turn on the **Toolbar**.

- ● You can switch between large and small icons, name-only and detailed lists to suit the job at hand.

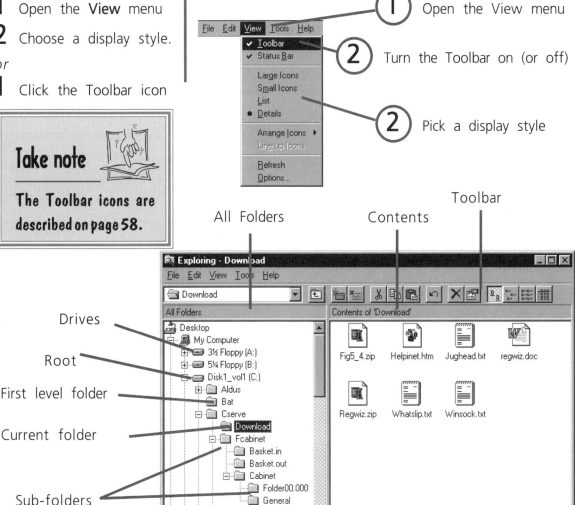

① Open the View menu

② Turn the Toolbar on (or off)

② Pick a display style

All Folders   Contents   Toolbar

Drives

Root

First level folder

Current folder

Sub-folders

Status line

Expanding folders

The *All Folders* tree can be shown in outline form, or with some or all of its branches shown in full.

The best display is always the simplest that will show you all you need. In most cases, this means most of the tree is collapsed back to its first level of main folders, with one or two branches expanded to show particular sub-folders. Now and then it is worth expanding the whole tree, just to get an idea of the overall structure and to see how sub-folders fit together.

If a folder has sub-folders, it will have a symbol beside it.

⊞   has sub-folders, and can be expanded

⊟   sub-folders displayed and can be collapsed.

❑ **To expand a folder**

1 Click the ⊞ by its name

2 Click the ⊞ by any sub-folders if you want to fully expand the whole branching set

❑ **To collapse a folder**

3 Click the ⊟ by its name

❑ **To collapse a whole branch**

4 Click the ⊟ by the folder at the top of the branched set

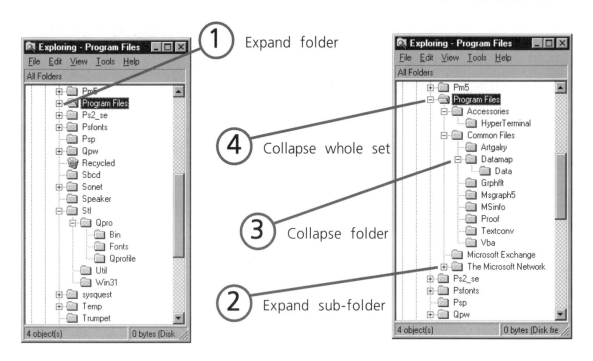

① Expand folder

④ Collapse whole set

③ Collapse folder

② Expand sub-folder

52

Basic steps

1 Point to the folder and click the right mouse button.

2 Select **Properties** from the short menu.

3 Wait for for the system to work out the total space and number of files.

4 Click ☒ to close the Properties panel.

Folder properties

Expanding a folder will show you what is in it, but not how much space all its files and folders occupy. The space report in the Status bar tells you how much is used by the files in the current folder only – not in its sub-folders. The total space figure can be important if you want to backup the folder, or copy it to floppies.

The Properties panel will tell us this – and other things.

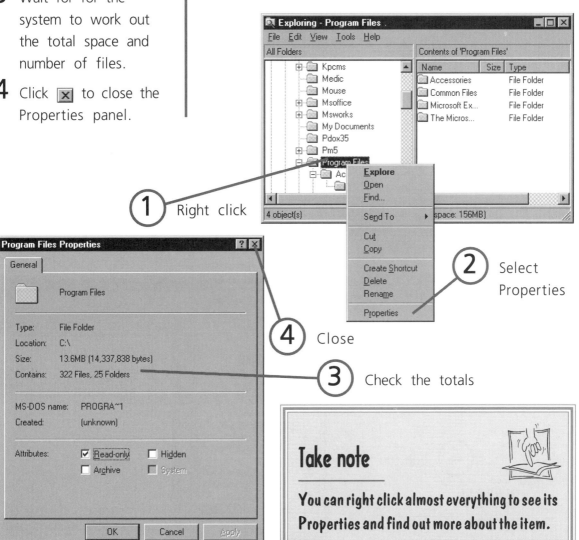

① Right click

② Select Properties

④ Close

③ Check the totals

Take note

You can right click almost everything to see its Properties and find out more about the item.

Creating a folder

Organised people set up their folders before they need them, so that they have places to store their letters – private and business, reports, memos, notes, and whatever, when they start to write them on their new system. They have a clear idea of the tree structure that they want, and create their folders at the right branches.

1 Select the folder that will be the parent of your new one, or the root if you want a new first level folder.

2 Open the **File** menu and point to **New** then select **Folder**

3 Open the **File** menu and select **Rename**

or

3 Click on the name twice – *separately*

4 Replace 'New Folder' with a new name – any length, any characters as with filenames.

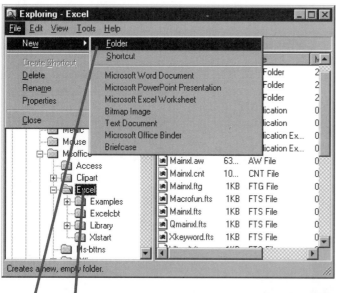

① Click on the parent

② Select File–New–Folder

③ Select File–Rename

④ Edit the name

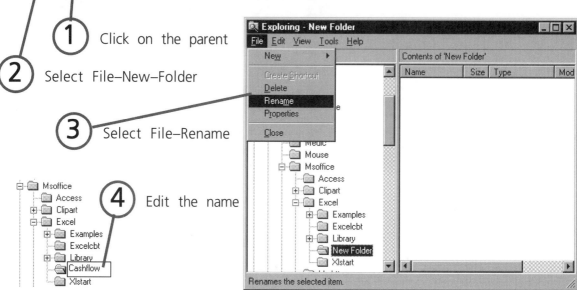

Basic steps

1 Arrange the display so that you can see the folder you want to move and the place it has to move to.

2 Drag the folder to its new position, *making sure the target is highlighted.*

Moving folders

Those of us who are less organised set up our new folders when the old ones get so full that it is difficult to find things. Nor do we always create them in the most suitable place in the tree. Fortunately, Windows 95 caters for us too. Files can easily be moved from one folder to another (See *Moving and copying*, page 66), and folders can easily be moved to new places on the tree.

In this example, *Cashflow* is being moved to its proper place as a branch of the *Excel* folder.

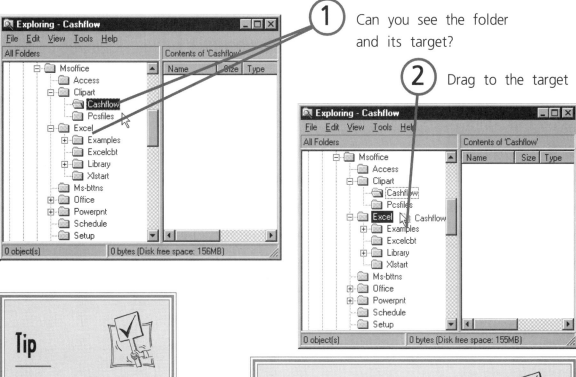

① Can you see the folder and its target?

② Drag to the target

Tip

Moving a folder – and all its files – to another disk can be a quick way to make a backup of a set of files.

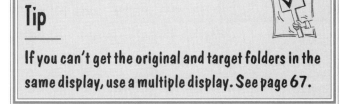

Tip

If you can't get the original and target folders in the same display, use a multiple display. See page 67.

Deleting folders

This is not something you will do every day, for deleting a folder also deletes its files, and files are usually precious things. But there are times. We all acquire programs we don't need, keep files long past their use-by dates, and sometimes create unnecessary folders.

● Don't worry about accidental deletions – files and folders deleted from your hard disk can be restored thanks to the Recycle bin. (See opposite.)

② Use File–Delete

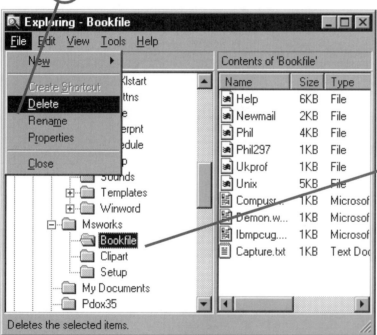

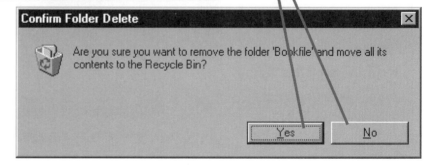

Basic steps

1 Select the folder – and check the files list. Are there any there? Do you want any of them? No, carry on.

2 Press [**Delete**] or select **Delete** from the **File** menu.

3 If necessary, you can stop the process by clicking **No** when you are asked to confirm that the folder is to be thrown in the bin.

① Select the folder

③ Confirm or stop

56

The Recycle Bin

1 Double click the Recycle Bin icon on the main desktop.

2 Select the files that were in the deleted folder – the **Original Location** field shows you where they were.

3 Open the **File** menu and select **Restore**

❑ The folder will be recreated and the files put back into it.

This is a wonderful feature, especially for those of us given to making instant decisions that we later regret. In Windows 95, deletions (from the hard disk) are done in two stages. The first stage is to throw the folder or file into the Recycle bin. The second stage is to empty the bin – and until you empty it, anything in the bin can be instantly restored.

② Select the files

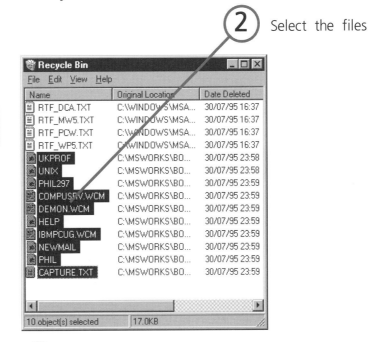

③ Use File–Restore

Take note

The Recycle Bin should be emptied regularly, to free up disk space. Check that there is nothing that you want then use File – Empty Recycle Bin.

Tip

If you don't know how to select groups of files, you can find out on page 64.

My Computer

At its default settings, the display of My Computer is simple, uncluttered and quite effective. You can see at a glance what files and folders are in the current folder – as long as there aren't too many! But sometimes, you need more control and more information.

Turn the Toolbar on, and you have instant access to some useful tools, plus a (limited) means of changing folders. The folder list on the Toolbar only shows the drives and the folders in the path from the root to the current one.

Switch to other drives or folders higher up the same path

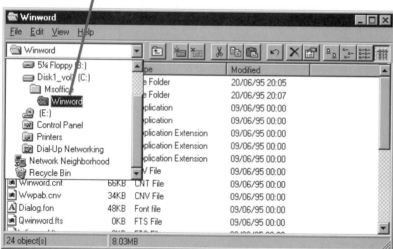

The Toolbar

🔼 Go to parent folder

📁 Map networked drives

📁 Disconnect from network

✂️ Cut – move folder or file to the Clipboard

📋 Copy file or folder to the Clipboard

📋 Paste from Clipboard into current folder

↩️ Undo last action

✖️ Delete file or folder

📄 Display properties of file or folder

🔲 Large icon file display

🔳 Small icon display

📋 Name only file list

📊 Detailed file list

Tip

The display can be adjusted in a number of ways – see Arranging icons, page 62.

Single window browsing

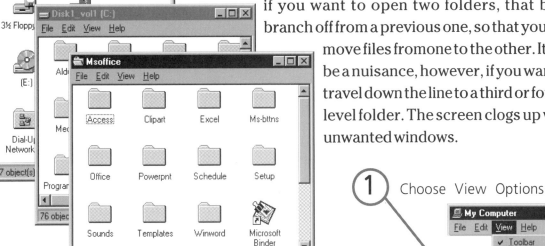

The main catch with the defaults is that each time you go into a new folder, it opens another window. This is useful if you want to open two folders, that both branch off from a previous one, so that you can move files from one to the other. It can be a nuisance, however, if you want to travel down the line to a third or fourth level folder. The screen clogs up with unwanted windows.

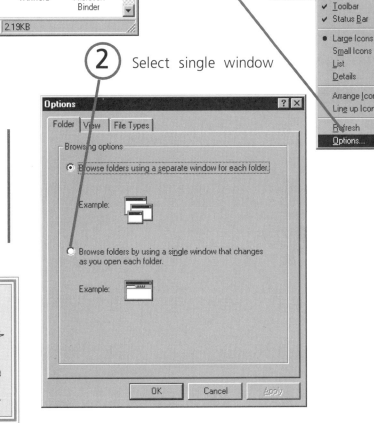

① Choose View Options

② Select single window

Basic steps

1 Open the **View** menu and select **Options**

2 On the **Folder** panel, switch to **Browse with single window**.

Take note

The other Options panels are covered on pages 73 and 80.

Summary

- ❏ You can use either **Explorer** or **My Computer** for managaing your files and folders.

- ❏ The Toolbar gives you quick access to all the commonly used commands.

- ❏ Disks are normally sub-divided into **folders**, to give organised storage for files.

- ❏ A folder's place in the tree is identified by its **path**.

- ❏ A **filename** has two components, the name itself and an extension.

- ❏ The **name** can be as long as you like, and contain any mixture of letters, digits and symbols.

- ❏ **Extensions** are used to identify the nature of the file.

- ❏ When you **create** a new folder, it will be placed on the branch below the selected folder.

- ❏ A folder, and its files, can be **moved** to a new position on the tree.

- ❏ A folder, and its files and sub-folders, can be deleted – but can be restored from the Recycle bin if necessary.

- ❏ **My Computer** can be set to run in a single or multiple windows.

60

6 Managing files

Arranging icons

Unless you specify otherwise, the Contents display lists your folders and files in alphabetical order – icons arranged across the screen; lists arranged in columns. Most of the time this works fine, but when you are moving or copying files, or hunting for them, other arrangements can be more convenient.

Basic steps

1 Open the **View** menu and point to **Arrange icons**

2 Select **by Name, Type, Size** or **Date**.

3 If it is the size or date that you are interested in, click 🏢 or use **View – Details** to get the full display.

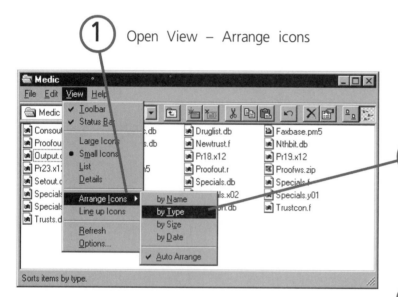

① Open View – Arrange icons

② Select the sort order

③ Use the Details display with Size or Date lists

Tip

If you need to free up some disk space and are looking for files to delete, use the Details display and arrange the icons by size or by Date – the biggest and oldest are at the end of the lists.

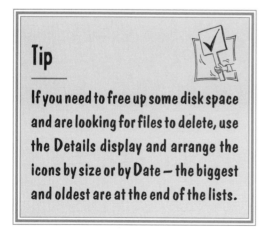

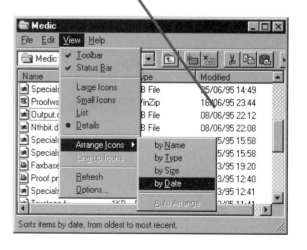

Basic steps

Improving visibility

□ **Adjusting Details**

1 Point the cursor at the dividing line between two field headings.

2 When the cursor changes to ↔, drag the dividing line to change the width of the field on its left.

□ **Adjusting the split**

3 Point anywhere on the bar between the panes to get the ↔ cursor.

4 Drag the shadowed line to adjust the relative size of the panes.

The amount of information in a My Computer or Explorer Contents display can vary greatly, depending upon the number of items in a folder and the display style. It is important that you should be able to adjust the display so that you can see things properly.

As well as being able to adjust the overall size of the window, you can also adjust the width of each field in a Details display, and the split between the All Folders and Contents panes of Explorer.

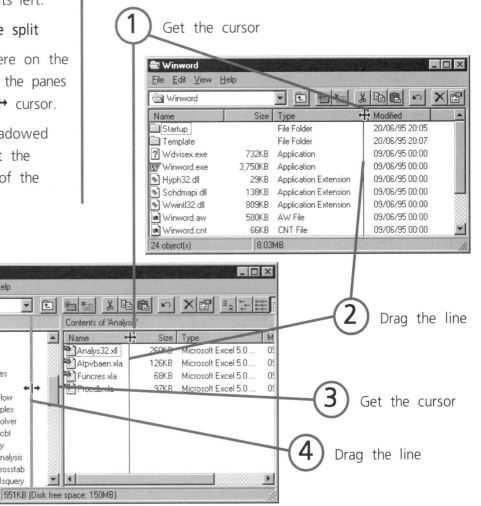

① Get the cursor

② Drag the line

③ Get the cursor

④ Drag the line

Selecting sets of files

You can easily select single files by clicking on them, but you can also select groups of files. This is useful when you want to backup a day's work by copying the new files to a floppy disk, or move a group from one folder to another, or delete a load of files that are not wanted.

You can select:

● a block of adjacent files;

● a scattered set;

● the whole folder-full.

The same techniques work in Explorer and My Computer, with all display styles.

Basic steps

❑ **To select a block using the mouse**

1 Point to one corner of the block

2 Drag an outline around the ones you want

❑ **[Shift] selecting**

1 Click on the file at one end of the block.

2 If necessary, scroll the window to bring the other end into view.

3 Hold **[Shift]** and click on the far end file.

❑ You can reselect the far end file to redefine the block.

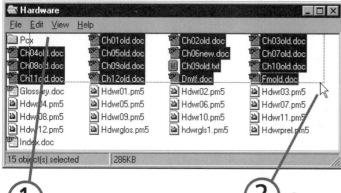

Press the mouse button — ① Press the mouse button ② Drag to enclose

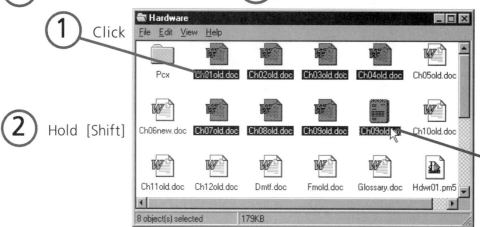

① Click
② Hold [Shift]
③ Click

Basic steps

❑ **To select scattered files**

1 Click on any one of the files you want.

2 Hold **[Ctrl]** and click each of the other files.

❑ You can deselect any file by clicking on it a second time.

❑ **To select all the files**

1 Open the **Edit** menu.

2 Choose **Select All**

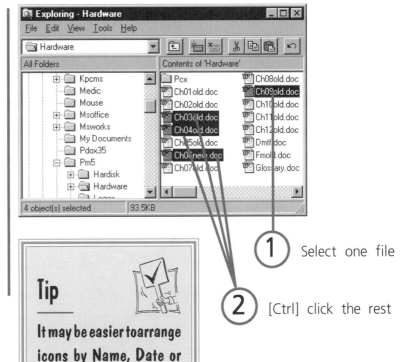

(1) Select one file

(2) [Ctrl] click the rest

Tip

It may be easier to arrange icons by Name, Date or Type, and [Shift] select.

(1) Open the Edit menu

(2) Choose Select All

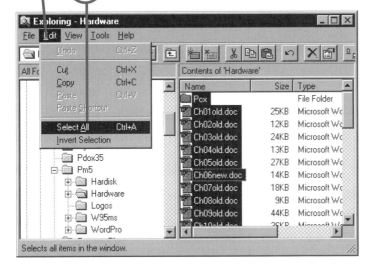

Tip

If you want all the files except for a scattered few, select them, then use Edit – Invert Selection to deselect them and select the others.

Moving and copying

When you drag a file from one place to another, it will either move or copy the file.

It is a **move** if you drag to somewhere *on the same disk.*

It is a **copy** if you drag the file *to a different disk.*

This is generally right. When you are dragging files within a disk, you are usually moving to reorganise your storage; and copying is most commonly to create a safe backup on a separate disk.

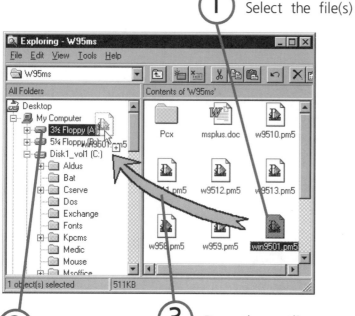

① Select the file(s)

② Scroll to see the folder or drive

③ Drag the outline

② Send the file to a floppy

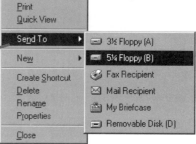

❑ **Moving within a disk**

1 Select the file(s).

2 Scroll the **All files** list so that you can see the destination folder – the **Contents** display will stay the same as long as you don't click on the destination.

3 Point to one of the selected files and drag to the destination.

❑ **Copying to a floppy**

Either

1 Follow the steps for moving, but drag the files to a floppy drive

or

1 Select the files

2 Open the **File** menu, point to **Send To** and select the destination drive

Basic steps

1 Open two Explorer or My Computer windows with one at the source and one at the destination folder.

2 Select the file(s).

3 Drag the files to their destination

Basic steps

1 Select the file(s)

2 *Move* with **Edit – Cut** or

2 *Copy* with **Edit – Copy**

3 Go to the destination drive or folder

4 Give the **Edit – Paste** command

Multiple windows

If you want to copy to a folder on a floppy, or you are having difficulty arranging the Explorer display so that you can see the source files and the target folder, the simplest approach is to use multiple windows. Use either Explorer or My Computer, or one of each.

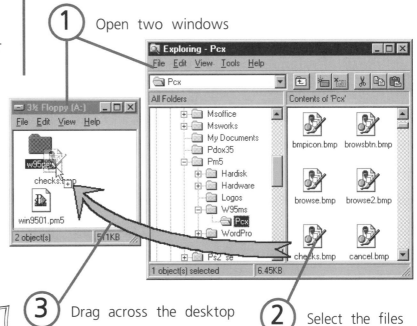

① Open two windows

③ Drag across the desktop

② Select the files

Using the Clipboard

Windows 95 allows you to move and copy files and folders, as well as text, graphics and other data, through an area of memory called the Clipboard.

The Cut, Copy and Paste commands are on the Edit menu of all Windows applications. Use them to copy within a disk, or move files to another disk – or for all your copying and moving, if you don't like dragging.

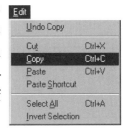

Special moves

For those times when you do want to copy within a disk or move to another, Windows 95 provides a special technique.

If you hold the *right* button down while you drag, a menu opens when the file reaches its destination.

1 Set up Explorer or My Computer windows so that you can see the source and destination folders.

2 Select the file(s).

3 Hold down the right button and drag the files across.

4 Select the **Move** or **Copy** action from the menu.

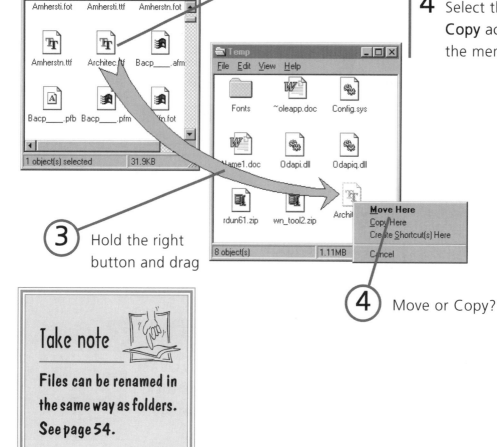

① Set up the windows

② Select the file(s)

③ Hold the right button and drag

④ Move or Copy?

Take note

Files can be renamed in the same way as folders. See page 54.

68

Basic steps

1 Select the file, or group of files.

2 Press [Delete].

3 At the Confirm prompt, click Yes or No to confirm or stop the deletion.

Deleting files

Thanks to the Recycle Bin, deleting files is no longer the dangerous occupation that it used to be – up to a point! Anything that you delete from the hard disk goes first into the bin, from which it can easily be recovered. Floppies are different. If you delete a file from a floppy it really does get wiped out, and the only way you might be able to recover it is by using the MS-DOS Undelete program.

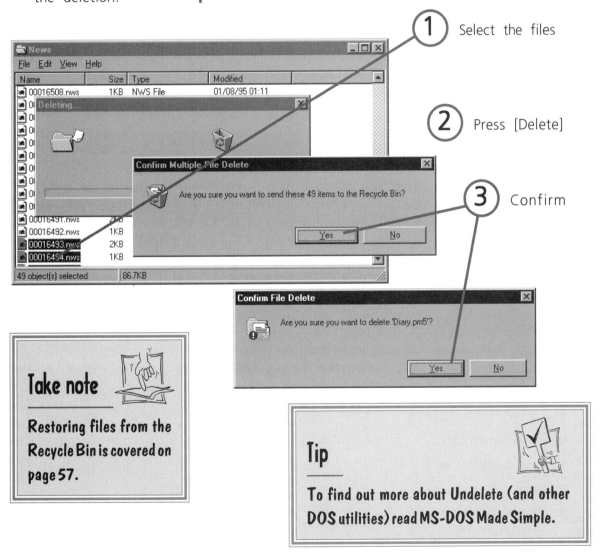

1 Select the files

2 Press [Delete]

3 Confirm

Take note

Restoring files from the Recycle Bin is covered on page 57.

Tip

To find out more about Undelete (and other DOS utilities) read MS-DOS Made Simple.

Finding files

If you are well organised, have a clear and logical structure of folders and consistently store your files in their proper places, then you should rarely need this facility when hunting outside your system. However, if you belong to the other 90% of users, you will be grateful for this.

- Find can track down files by name, type, age, size or contents. As long as you have something to go on, no files need remain lost for long.

- You can run Find either from Explorer or from the Start menu.

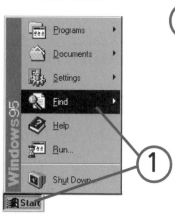

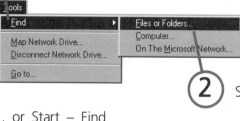

① Use either Tools – Find …

② Select Files or Folders

.. or Start – Find

Take note

The other Find options lead to different panels, to find a Computer on a network, or a service on the Microsoft Network

Partial names and Wildcards

If you just type part of a name into the Named slot, Find will track down any file with those characters anywhere in the name.

e.g. *'DOC'* will find 'My *Doc*uments', 'Letter to *doc*tor', and all Word files with a *.DOC* extension.

If you know the start of the name and the extension, fill the gap with the wildcard *. (include the dot!)

e.g. *REP*.TXT* will find '*REP*ORT MAY 15.*TXT*', '*REP*LY TO IRS.*TXT*' and similar files.

3 Type as much of the name as you know into the **Named** slot

4 Select the drive from the **Look in** list or click Browse if you want to restrict the search to a particular folder.

5 Click [Find Now]

6 If the file you want is not in the list, try one of the other methods (see next page)

If it is there..

Either

7 Double click the file to run it, or open it with its associated program

or

8 Click to select it and pull down the **File** menu. This has most of the Explorer filing options on it, and also allows you to open the file's folder.

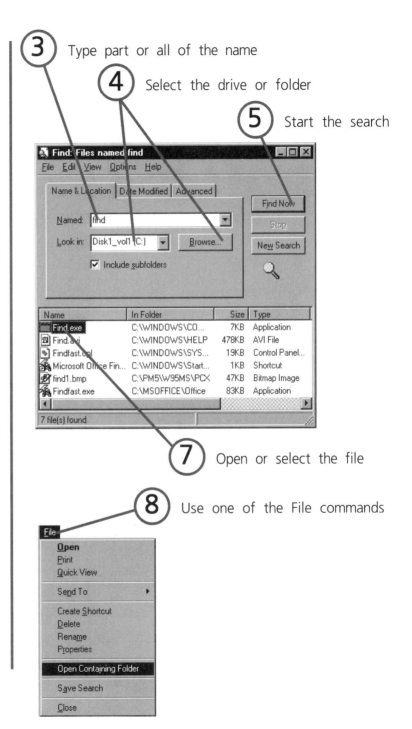

(3) Type part or all of the name

(4) Select the drive or folder

(5) Start the search

(7) Open or select the file

(8) Use one of the File commands

71

Finding by date

If you know when you last created or edited the file, but not its name, use the Date Modified tab to set the **between** limits or a **previous days** or **months** limit.

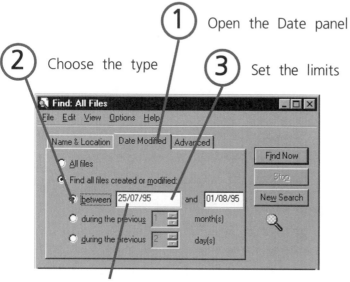

① Open the Date panel

② Choose the type

③ Set the limits

Enter dates as numbers in Day/Month/Year order; e.g. 24/08/95 for 24th August 1995

Advanced searches

You can focus the search by specifying the File type, or a minimum or maximum size. With text files, you can also give a key word or phrase.

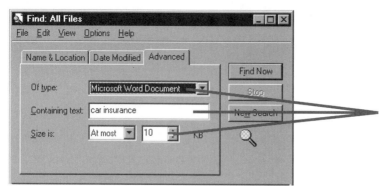

1 Click the **Date Modified** tab to open the panel

2 Select the type of search – **between**, **months** or **days**.

3 Set the limits.

4 Start the search or go to another panel

Tip

When finding by date, restrict the search to a selected folder or by setting **Advanced** criteria, to reduce the number of files in the output list.

Specifying one or more of these helps to focus the search

Basic steps

1 Open the **View** menu.

2 Select **Options**

3 Click the tab to open the **View** panel

4 Select **Show all files**

5 Click [OK]

The normal display does not necessarily show every file that is in a folder, for there are some types that you do not usually need to see and which are safer out of the way.

● **Application extensions** – files with **.DLL** extensions. They add extra features to applications.

● **System files** – marked by **.SYS** after the name. These are essential to Windows 95's internal workings.

● **Drivers** – with **.VXD**, **.386** or **.DRV** extensions. These are the files that make printers, screens, mice and other hardware work properly.

The WINDOWS and WINDOWS/SYSTEM folders are full of them. You can see them by changing the View Options.

Take note

If you remove an application or change part of your hardware, you might want to delete the related **DLL** or driver files – in which case, you must be able to see them. But don't delete any file unless you are certain it is no longer needed.

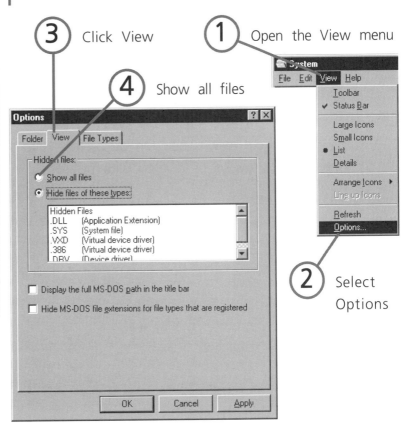

③ Click View

① Open the View menu

④ Show all files

② Select Options

Summary

- ❏ You can **arrange icons** by Name, Type, Size or Date.

- ❏ Files and folders can be displayed as **icons** or in **lists with details**.

- ❏ You can use [Shift] to **select a block of files**, or [Ctrl] to **select a scattered set**. A block of files can also be selected with the mouse.

- ❏ **Dragging a file** will normally move it within the disk, or copy it to a floppy.

- ❏ By holding the **right button** as you drag, you can copy within a disk or move to a floppy.

- ❏ To **delete** a file, press [Delete]. If the file was on the hard disk, it is sent to the Recycle Bin, fromwhich it can be recovered.

- ❏ The **Find** utility will help you to track down files if you have forgotten where you put them, or what they were called.

- ❏ Those files that are essential to the system are usually hidden from view. They can be brought into view, but should always be treated with respect.

7 Programs and files

Properties

As we saw on page 21, everything in Windows 95 has Properties. If you open the Properties box for any file, you will see a General panel, containing information about the file and some controls. Some files have additional panels.

● Program files have Version panels carrying product details;

● Word-processor, spreadsheet and other data files created by newer applications have Summary and Statistics panels. Summary information is created by the application's user to describe the contents of the file; the Statistics include the number of pages, words, characters and the like, and the dates when the file was created, last modified or accessed.

● Shortcuts have their own special panels (see next pages)

1 Select the file and click the 🖾 Tool

or

1 Right click the file and select **Properties** from the short menu.

2 If you want to prevent the file from being edited, tick the **Read Only** checkbox.

3 Click tabs to open other panels, if present

4 Click ▭ OK ▭ or ☒ to close.

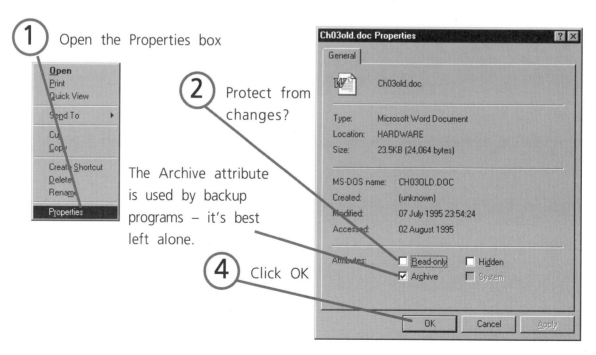

① Open the Properties box

② Protect from changes?

The Archive attribute is used by backup programs – it's best left alone.

④ Click OK

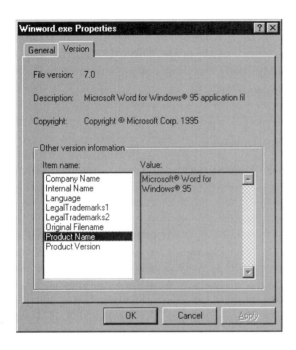

The **Version** panel (left) can tell you more about when and by whom a program was created. As its name implies, it is particularly useful for checking which version of a program you have.

The **Summary** panel (below) displays information written into it while the file was open in its application.

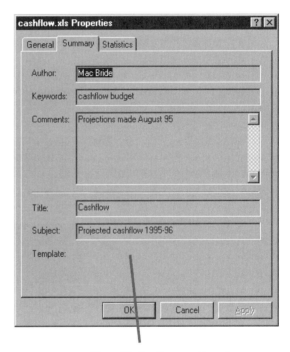

The file's Properties box displayed from Explorer

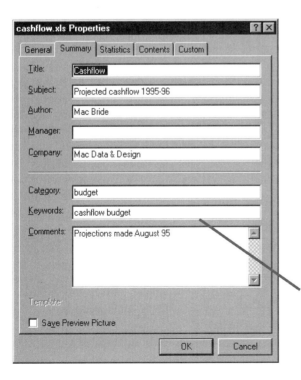

The file's Properties box opened for editing in Excel.

Shortcuts

You can run a program by double-clicking on its EXE file in Explorer or My Computer, but Shortcuts make it easier. Shortcuts can be added to the Start menu (see page 106) or placed directly on the desktop. This is a very convenient way of running programs that you use regularly.

You can set up a shortcut in less than a minute – and if you find that you are not really making much use of it, you can remove a shortcut even faster!

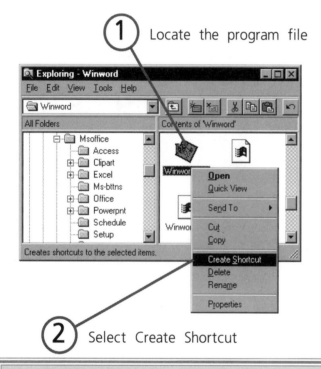

① Locate the program file

② Select Create Shortcut

Take note

Too many shortcuts will clutter up your Desktop.

Remove excess ones by selecting them and pressing [Delete]. This does not remove the program – only the shortcut.

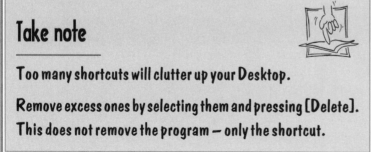

Basic steps

1 Use **Explorer** or **My Computer** to find the program file – it will have an EXE, or possibly COM extension.

2 Right click the file to open its short menu and select **Create Shortcut**

3 If you are running Explorer Maximized, reduce it to **Restore** mode, so that you can see the Desktop.

4 Find the new Shortcut icon in the program's folder.

5 Drag the Shortcut icon onto the desktop

6 Edit the name to remove 'Shortcut to..'

7 Open the icon's **Properties** box and click the **Shortcut** tab.

8 Change the **Start in** folder, **Run** mode or **Icon** as required

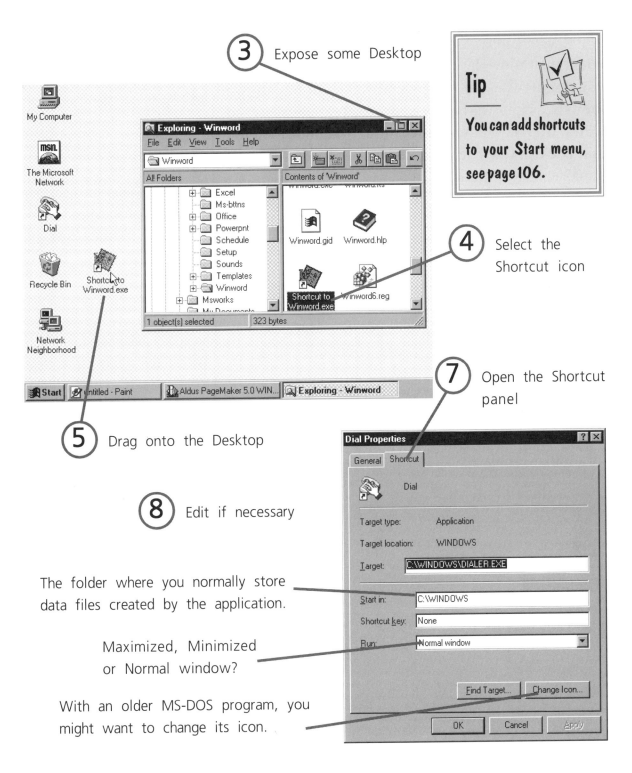

③ Expose some Desktop

Exploring - Winword

File Edit View Tools Help

Winword

All Folders | Contents of 'Winword'

⊞ Excel
Ms-bttns
⊞ Office
⊞ Powerpnt
Schedule
Setup
Sounds
⊞ Templates
⊞ Winword
⊞ Msworks
My Documents

Winword.gid   Winword.hlp

Shortcut to   Winword6.reg
Winword.exe

1 object(s) selected | 323 bytes

My Computer

The Microsoft Network

Dial

Recycle Bin   Shortcut to Winword.exe

Network Neighborhood

Start | untitled - Paint | Aldus PageMaker 5.0 WIN... | Exploring - Winword

Tip

You can add shortcuts to your Start menu, see page 106.

④ Select the Shortcut icon

⑦ Open the Shortcut panel

⑤ Drag onto the Desktop

⑧ Edit if necessary

The folder where you normally store data files created by the application.

Maximized, Minimized or Normal window?

With an older MS-DOS program, you might want to change its icon.

Dial Properties

General | Shortcut

Dial

Target type: Application

Target location: WINDOWS

Target: C:\WINDOWS\DIALER.EXE

Start in: C:\WINDOWS

Shortcut key: None

Run: Normal window

Find Target...   Change Icon...

OK   Cancel   Apply

79

File types

Windows 95 keeps a list of registered file types. These are ones that it knows how to describe and how to handle. If you double-click on, or open, a document of a known type, the system will run the appropriate application and load in the file. Windows 95 comes with a good long list, and you can teach it about new types through one of Explorer's View options.

1 Open the **View** menu and select **Options**..

2 Click the **File Types** tab to open its panel

3 Click New Type...

4 Type in a **Description**

5 Enter the **Extension**(s) that mark this type

6 You must define the Actions that can be performed on this file. Click New...

7 In the **Action** slot, type '*open*'

8 Go to the application slot then Browse... through your folders and select it

9 Close and OK back to the main panel

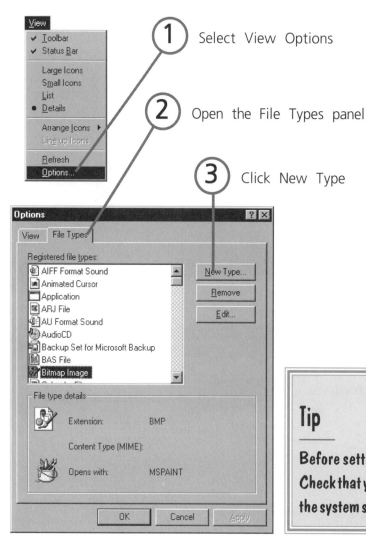

① Select View Options

② Open the File Types panel

③ Click New Type

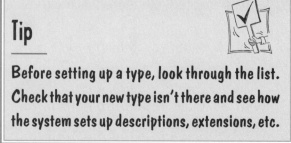

Tip

Before setting up a type, look through the list. Check that your new type isn't there and see how the system sets up descriptions, extensions, etc.

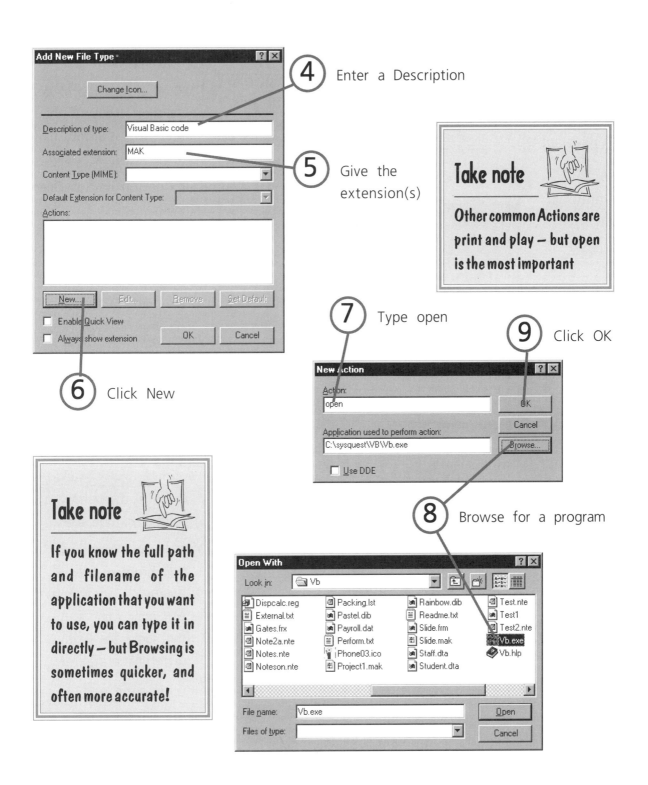

④ Enter a Description

⑤ Give the extension(s)

Take note

Other common Actions are print and play – but open is the most important

⑦ Type open

⑨ Click OK

⑥ Click New

Take note

If you know the full path and filename of the application that you want to use, you can type it in directly – but Browsing is sometimes quicker, and often more accurate!

⑧ Browse for a program

Open With...

The View Options File Type panel offers a thorough, if slightly long-winded, means of registering new types. A rough and ready alternative is to simply tell Windows what program to use as and when you try to open unknown types of files.

Basic steps

❑ Opening With ..

1 Right click a file to get its short menu. If the first item is **Open**, no steps need be taken.

2 If the top item is **Open With..**, select it.

3 At the **Open With** dialog box, type a **Description**. This will be used in Details displays in Explorer

4 Scroll through the list and pick the program to use with this file.

5 If you can't find the program in the list click ⬚ Other... ⬚ and browse through your folders to find it.

6 Tick the **Always use this program** box, if wanted – sometimes you may want to use the same file with different programs.

7 Click ⬚ OK ⬚

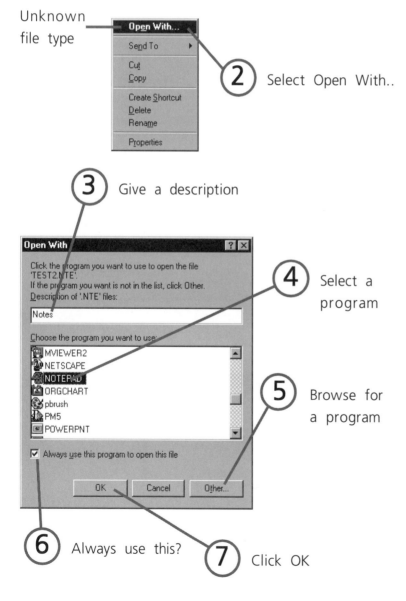

Unknown file type

Open With...
Send To ▶
Cut
Copy
Create Shortcut
Delete
Rename
Properties

② Select Open With..

③ Give a description

Open With ? ✕

Click the program you want to use to open the file 'TEST2.NTE'.
If the program you want is not in the list, click Other.
Description of '.NTE' files:
[Notes]

Choose the program you want to use:

MVIEWER2
NETSCAPE
NOTEPAD
ORGCHART
pbrush
PM5
POWERPNT

☑ Always use this program to open this file

[OK] [Cancel] [Other...]

④ Select a program

⑤ Browse for a program

⑥ Always use this?

⑦ Click OK

Basic steps

1 Select the type

2 Click [Edit...]

Either

3 Select an action and click [Edit...] to link a new program

or

4 Change the icon

or

5 Turn Quick View on or off

Editing a type

Whether you set up your new type through the View Options, or through Open With, it is possible that it may need some fine tuning later. You may want to change its icon, or turn Quick View (see overleaf) on or off.

Established file types may also need editing over time as you replace programs with newer versions, but still retain the data files.

The Edit panel is reached through View Options.

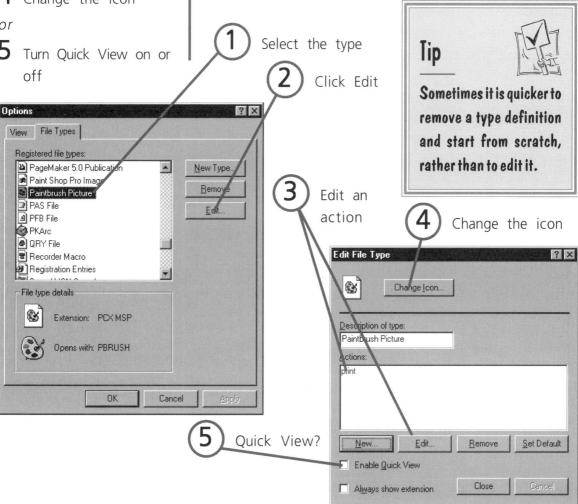

① Select the type

② Click Edit

Tip

Sometimes it is quicker to remove a type definition and start from scratch, rather than to edit it.

③ Edit an action

④ Change the icon

⑤ Quick View?

Quick View

You will appreciate this facility if, like me, you cannot always identify a file by its name – time passes and we forget. As the name suggests, it gives a means of taking a quick look at a document. Typically it is three to four times faster to open a document in Quick View than in its original application.

Not all document files will work with Quick View, but you can view any Microsoft Office spreadsheet, presentation, database or Word file, bitmaps, more or less any text file, and some others. It seems to cover documents from most of the big, new applications – the ones that take so long to load – and those are the ones that matter most.

1 Locate the file with **Explorer** or **My Computer**.

2 Right click to open the short menu.

3 If **Quick View** is present, select it.

4 Click the program icon or select Open File for Editing from the short menu if you wan to edit it.

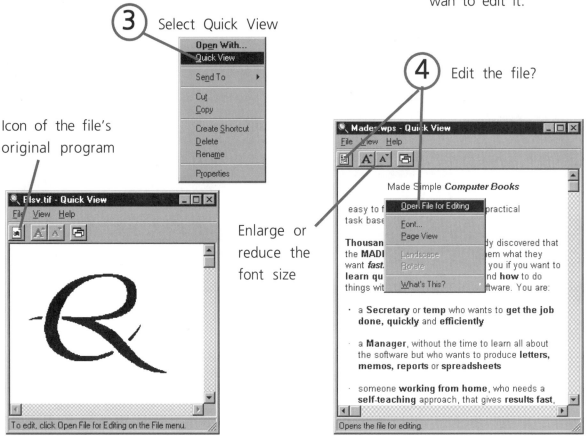

③ Select Quick View

Icon of the file's original program

Enlarge or reduce the font size

④ Edit the file?

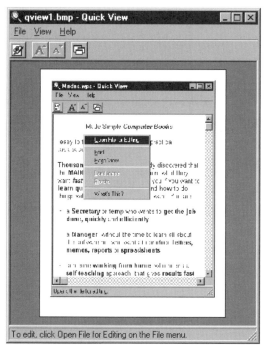

Quick View options

As well as **Open File for Editing**, the short menu offers:

Page view – probably the most useful;

Landscape – shows how the document would fit on paper, if turned sideways;

Rotate – turns the document through a quarter circle (!);

Font – lets you choose the style and size of text.

Take note

Once Quick View is open, you can drag other files onto it for viewing.

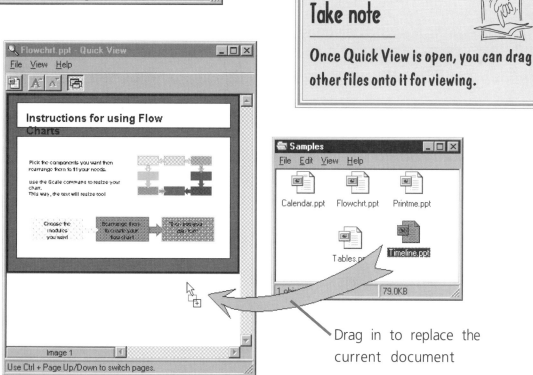

Drag in to replace the current document

Summary

❑ The **Properties** box of a file can be a useful source of information.

❑ You can create **Shortcuts** to programs and place them on your desktop for quick and easy access.

❑ If Windows 95 knows about a **file type**, it knows how to describe it and what program to open it with. You can teach the system about new types.

❑ When you try to open a file of an unknown type, you will get the **Open With..** option and can then tell it which program to use.

❑ The **Quick View** utility can be a convenient way of checking through your documents.

8 Disk housekeeping

The system tools

Windows 95 comes equipped with a set of disk housekeeping tools – programs that help to keep your disks in good condition, and your data safe.

Scandisk – finds and fixes errors in data stored on disks

Defrag – optimises the disk's speed and efficiency

Backup – provides a means of creating safe and compact backup copies of your files

Drivespace – allows you to double the capacity of disks

Inbox Repair tool – fixes any errors in your mail files.

Resource Meter – runs minimized in the background. Right click on its icon on the Taskbar, to see what percentages of your system's resources are in use.

System Monitor – lets you examine the performance of different aspects of the system.

Basic steps

1 Click ⊞Start

2 Point to **Programs**

3 Point to **Accessories**

4 Point to **System Tools**

5 Click to select a tool

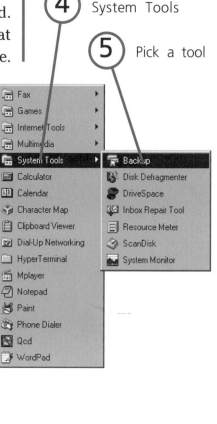

④ System Tools

⑤ Pick a tool

③ Accessories

② Programs

① Click Start

88

Basic steps

1 Open **My Computer** and right click on the drive you want to work on

2 Bring the **Tools** tab to the front

3 Select a tool

Routine chores

The three system tools that are needed for the routine housekeeping chores can also be reached from the Properties box of any disk. The messages will remind you of chores you have been neglecting!

① Right click on C:

② Open the Tools panel

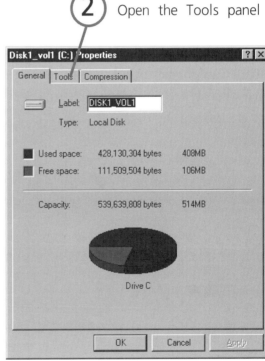

This is Scandisk

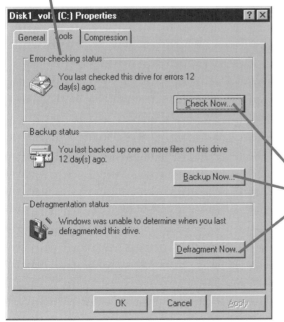

③ Pick a tool

89

Scandisk

Data is stored on disks in *allocation units.* A small file may fit on a single unit, but others are spread over many. A file's units may be in a continuous run or scattered over the disk (see *Disk Defragmenter,* page 96), but are kept together by links from one to the next. Sometimes these links get corrupted leaving *Lost fragments,* with no known links to any file, or *Cross-linked files,* where two are chained to the same unit of data. Scandisk can find – and often fix – these problems.

Sometimes the magnetic surface of the disk becomes corrupted, creating *Bad sectors* where data cannot be stored safely. Scandisk can identify these and, with a bit of luck, retrieve any data written there and transfer it to a safe part of the disk.

② Select a drive ③ Standard or Thorough?

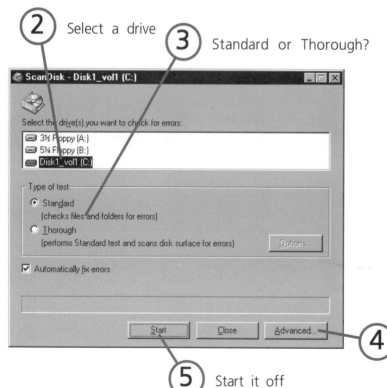

⑤ Start it off

④ Open the Advanced box

Basic steps

1 Run **Scandisk** from the Start menu or the disk's Properties box.

2 Select the **Drive** to be scanned

3 Normally go for the quicker **Standard** scan, to fix file errors only. Do a **Thorough** scan to check for bad sectors on new disks and then every couple of months.

4 Set **Advanced** options as required – see opposite.

5 Click [Start]

Take note

If the Standard scan finds bad sectors, it will offer to run a Thorough scan to fix them.

90

Advanced options

The *Summary* is always worth having.

Turn off the *log* if you don't use it.

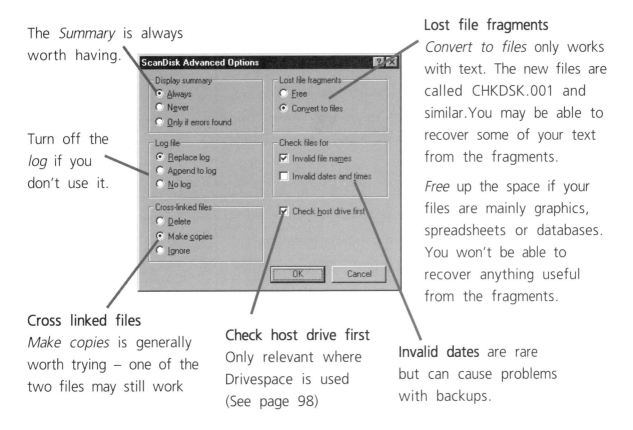

Lost file fragments
Convert to files only works with text. The new files are called CHKDSK.001 and similar.You may be able to recover some of your text from the fragments.

Free up the space if your files are mainly graphics, spreadsheets or databases. You won't be able to recover anything useful from the fragments.

Cross linked files
Make copies is generally worth trying – one of the two files may still work

Check host drive first
Only relevant where Drivespace is used (See page 98)

Invalid dates are rare but can cause problems with backups.

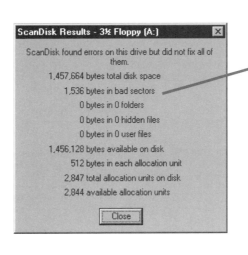

Scandisk has found bad sectors on this floppy. It has also prevented future errors by marking them off so that they are not used.

Tip

If you want to know more about Scandisk, see Hard Drives Made Simple.

Backup

Modern hard disks are very reliable, but they can all develop problems eventually – some sooner than others. Making safe backup copies of your documents should be part of your regular routines.

- Do a full backup of the C: drive after installing Windows 95, and again later after any major changes.

- Backup your document files after you have done a substantial amount of work – this may mean every day, or once a month, depending upon your activity.

With partial backups, you should filter out all the irrelevant files – exclude every type except those of documents that you have created.

Basic steps

1 Run **Backup** from the Start menu or the disk's Properties box.

2 For a **Full backup**, select Drive C: and go to step **7**

3 Open the **Settings** menu and select **File Filtering**

4 In the **File Types**, click [Select All], then work through the list and deselect your document types

5 Click [Exclude] then [OK] to return to the main dialog box.

6 Select single files or whole folders of files to be backed up

7 Click [Next Step >]

8 Select the **Device**– and folder if appropriate – to hold the backup.

9 Click [Start Backup]

10 Give a name for the backup file

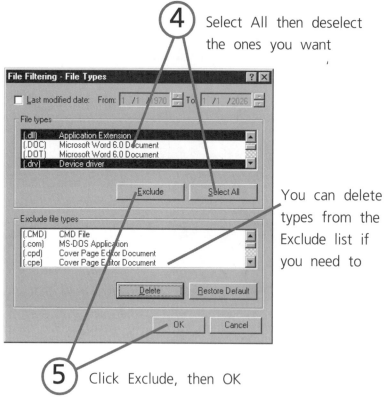

④ Select All then deselect the ones you want

You can delete types from the Exclude list if you need to

⑤ Click Exclude, then OK

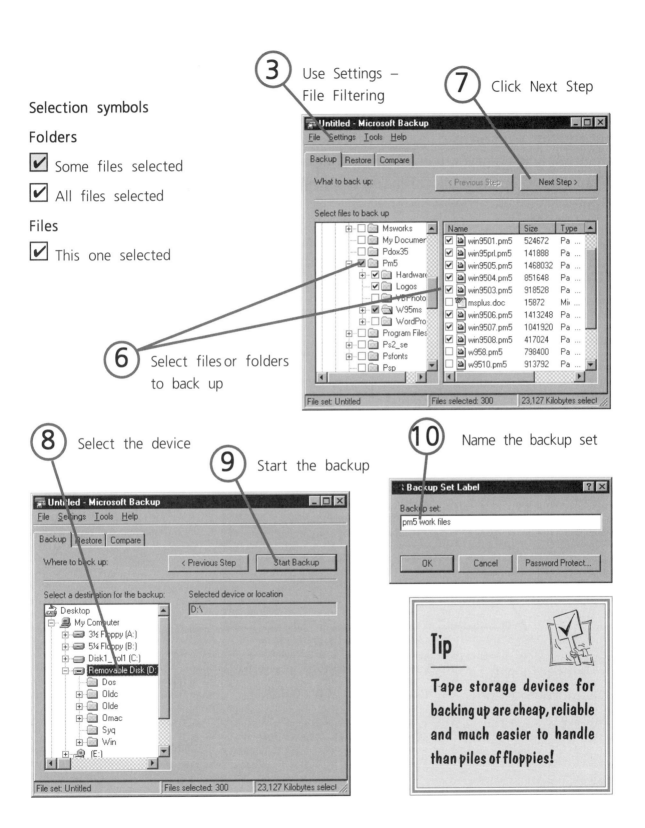

Selection symbols

Folders

☑ Some files selected

☑ All files selected

Files

☑ This one selected

③ Use Settings –
File Filtering

⑦ Click Next Step

⑥ Select files or folders
to back up

⑧ Select the device

⑨ Start the backup

⑩ Name the backup set

Tip

Tape storage devices for backing up are cheap, reliable and much easier to handle than piles of floppies!

Backup options

Do make sure that **data compression** is turned on. This almost always saves space – though the backup control information adds an overhead, so that the backup of a single file may be larger than the original! Some types of files can be compressed more than others. Typical space-savings:

Programs 25%; Text files 33%; Graphics 75%

Take note

If you want to backup the same set of files regularly, save the set definition with the command File – Save As. Next time you want to backup the same files, use File – Open File Set to load in the definition.

Saves having to close down Backup after it has done

Use *Full* the first time you save a set of files.

Use *Incremental* for later backups of the same set.

Turn this on!

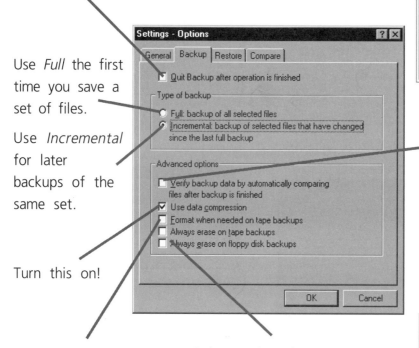

Turn on verification if you have limited faith in the quality of your backup tapes/disks.

Automatic formatting is a convenience for tape users

Only set the Always erase options if you are confident you will not try to save over a backup file that you want

Tip

There's lots more about Backup in Hard Drives Made Simple

Basic steps

1 Run **Backup** and click the **Restore** tab to open its panel.

2 Select the **Device**, then the **Backup set**.

3 Click **Next Step**.

4 Pick the files you wnat to restore.

5 Click **Start Restore**.

With any luck, you will never have to restore a lost file. However, should you need to, it's a simple process.

① Open the Restore panel

③ Click Next Step

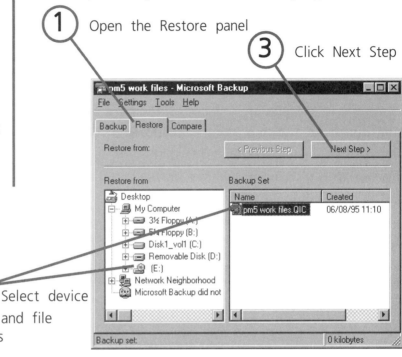

② Select device and file

④ Select the files

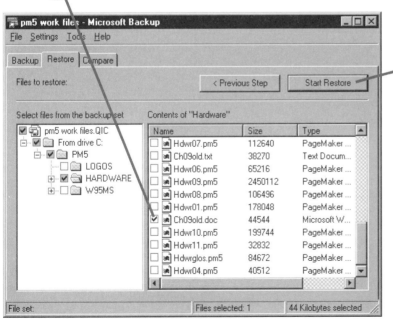

⑤ Start the Restore

Tip

If you want to check that the backup is accurate, use the **Compare** panel. The steps are almost identical to Restore.

Disk Defragmenter

When you first start to write data onto a disk, the files go on, one after the other, with each occupying a continuous run of disk space. When you access one of these files, the drive simply finds the start point, then reads the data in a single sweep.

After the disk has been in use for some time, holes begin to appear in the layout, and not all files are stored in a continuous area. Some have been deleted, others will have grown during editing, so that they no longer fit in their original slot, but now have parts stored elsewhere on the disk. When you store a new file, there may not be a single space large enough for it, and it is stored in scattered sections. The drive is becoming *fragmented*. The data is still safe, but the access speed will suffer as the drive now has to hunt for each fragment of the file.

Basic steps

1 Run the **Defragmenter** from the Start menu or the disk's Properties box.

2 Select the drive.

3 Check the status.

4 If the fragmentation is over 10%, click **Start**

   Under 5%, click **Exit**

   In between, do it if you have spare time.

5 When defragmenting starts, click **Show Details** to see what's going on.

6 Go and make a cuppa – it can take up to an hour to defragment a large drive.

② Select a drive

Select Drive   ? ☒

Which drive do you want to defragment?

- 🖴 Disk1_vol1 (C:) ▼
- 🖴 5¼ Floppy (B:)
- 🖴 Disk1_vol1 (C:)
- 🖴 Removable Disk (D:)

   OK   Exit

③ Check the state

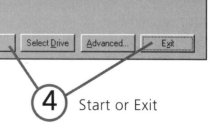

④ Start or Exit

⑤ Show Details to see it at work

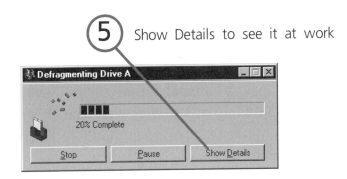

The Legend shows what the coloured squares mean

Watching the Defragmenter at work is more exciting than watching paint dry, but not much.

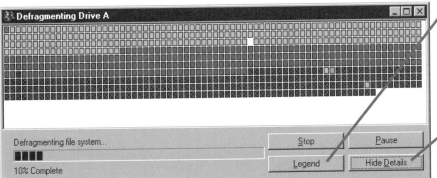

Advanced options

The defaults are usually right. Change them only if essential.

Improves access times on existing files, but new files may be scattered.

New files will be stored efficiently, but existing ones remain fragmented.

Check if you haven't run Scandisk recently.

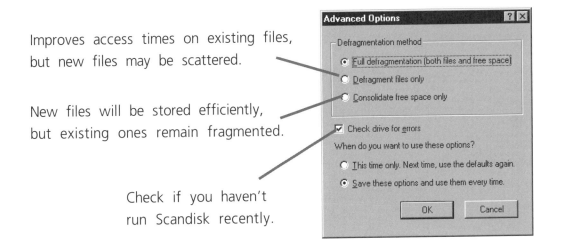

DriveSpace

It seems that every new version of every application that comes along takes up more disk space than the last. Only a few years ago a 40Mb hard disk would have more than enough capacity for most people, but now even a 500Mb disk soon fills up. It's just as well that DriveSpace is around. This stores files in a compressed form and can almost double the capacity of a disk.

You can compress floppy disks, boosting their capacity to around 2.6Mb. This is certainly worth doing if you back up onto floppies.

Installing it on your hard disk is a slow process, but you only have to do it once!

Basic steps

1 Run **DriveSpace**

2 Select the disk to be compressed.

3 Open the **Drive** menu and select **Compress**.

4 You will see an estimate of the space gain. The actual gain will depend upon the types of files on your disk, as some can be compressed more than others. If the gain is worthwhile – and it should be – click Start

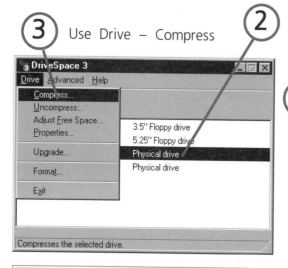

③ Use Drive – Compress

② Select a drive

④ Click Start

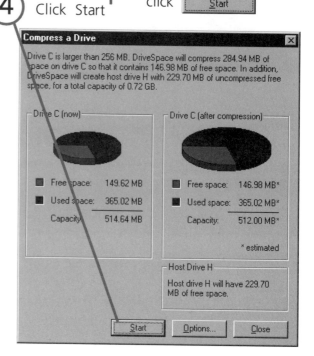

Take note

You can also run DriveSpace from the Compression panel of a drive's Properties box.

5 If you have not backed up the disk recently, take the offer to do so now – there's a very slight possibility that files could get corrupted.

6 Click [Compress Now] and put your feet up for a while.

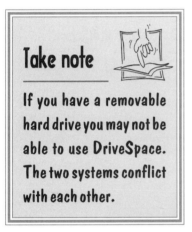

Take note

If you have a removable hard drive you may not be able to use DriveSpace. The two systems conflict with each other.

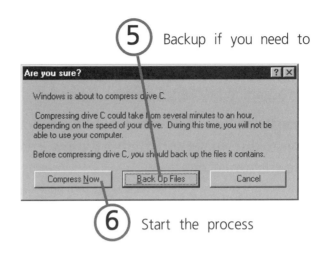

(5) Backup if you need to

Are you sure? [?][X]

Windows is about to compress drive C.

Compressing drive C could take from several minutes to an hour, depending on the speed of your drive. During this time, you will not be able to use your computer.

Before compressing drive C, you should back up the files it contains.

[Compress Now] [Back Up Files] [Cancel]

(6) Start the process

DriveSpace3

DriveSpace2 is limited to 512Mb in the size of compressed drives it can create – using about 250Mb of uncompressed drive. If wanted any remaining uncomressed space can be made into a second drive.

DriveSpace3, part of the Microsoft Plus! package, has no such limit – it can compress drives of any size. It can also compress them more tightly! Compare its report, here, with that of DriveSpace 2, opposite.

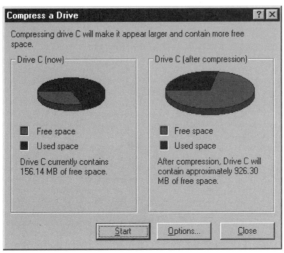

Compress a Drive [?][X]

Compressing drive C will make it appear larger and contain more free space.

Drive C (now)
Drive C (after compression)

■ Free space
■ Used space

Drive C currently contains 156.14 MB of free space.

■ Free space
■ Used space

After compression, Drive C will contain approximately 926.30 MB of free space.

[Start] [Options...] [Close]

Tip

DriveSpace is covered in more detail in Hard Drives Made Simple

Formatting a floppy

Before you can use a new floppy disk, it is must be **formatted**. This marks out magnetic tracks on the disk surface, dividing the area up into numbered blocks to provide organised storage space.

The **Format** command takes the hard work out of this – all you have to do is make sure that you know what kind of disk you are formatting.

PC disks come in two sizes and four capacities.

5.25 inch	360Kb Double-Density (DD)
5.25 inch	1.2Mb High-Density (HD)
3.5 inch	720Kb Double-Density (DD)
3.5 inch	1.44Mb High-Density (HD)

PCs are normally fitted with 3.5" drives, that can take either capacity. The 1.44Mb disk is better value for money.

Basic steps

1 Insert the disk into the drive.

2 Run **My Computer** or **Explorer**.

3 Open the **Properties** menu and select **Format**.

4 At the dialog box, make sure that it is set for the right disk size.

5 Select **Full**

6 Click [Start]

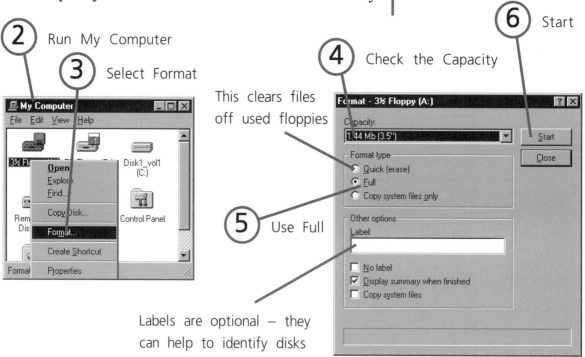

Run My Computer

Select Format

Check the Capacity

Start

This clears files off used floppies

Use Full

Labels are optional – they can help to identify disks

100

Caring for floppies

❏ Disk drives can be mounted horizontally or vertically, but a disk will only go in one way round. If it won't fit, don't force it. Try it the other way round.

The modern 3.5" floppy is a far tougher beast than the older 5.25" ones. Its plastic casing protects it well against grime, knocks and splashes of coffee, but it still has enemies. Heat, damp and magnetism will both go through the casing and corrupt the data on the disk beneath. So, keep your disks away from radiators, sunny windowsills, magnets, heavy electrical machinery or mains cables – both produce magnetic fields.

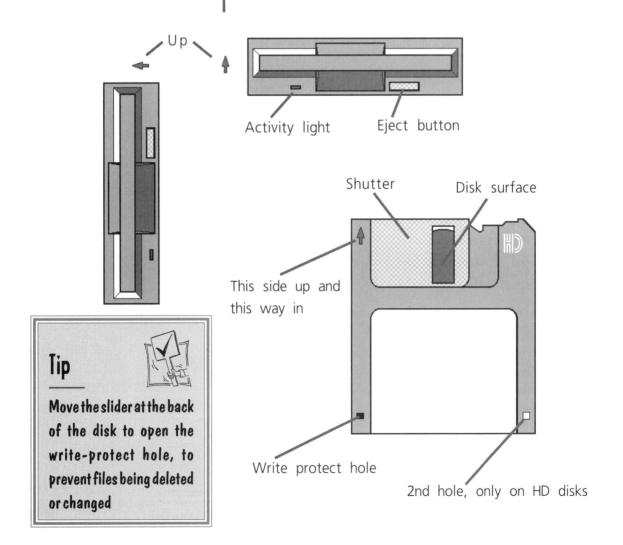

Up

Activity light   Eject button

Shutter   Disk surface

This side up and this way in

Tip

Move the slider at the back of the disk to open the write-protect hole, to prevent files being deleted or changed

Write protect hole

2nd hole, only on HD disks

Summary

❑ Windows 95 is supplied with a set of very useful **system tools**.

❑ **Scandisk** can find and fix errors on your disks.

❑ **Backup** provides a simple and efficient way of creating backup copies of your files. The backups are compressed, significantly saving space.

❑ If you lose backed up files, they can be recovered using **Restore**.

❑ The **Disk Defragmenter** should be run regularly to ensure that files are stored compactly, and can therefore be loaded faster.

❑ **DriveSpace** can more or less double the effective capacity of a floppy or hard disk.

❑ **DriveSpace3**, part of the Microsoft Plus set, can handle very large hard disks.

❑ Floppy disks must be fully **formatted** before they can be used.

❑ If you want to reuse a disk with old files on it, the **Quick Format** option is the fastest way to erase files.

❑ Floppies should be **stored safely** away from heat, damp and sources of magnetism.

9 The Taskbar

Taskbar options

Many parts of the Windows 95 system can be tailored to your own needs and tastes. Some of the most important are covered in the next three sections. We'll start with the Taskbar and the Start menu.

You can adjust the size of the Taskbar icons, turn the clock on or off, hide the Taskbar, or place it on any edge of the screen.

❑ Adjusting the display

1 Click **Start**

2 Point to **Settings**

3 Click on **Taskbar..**

4 Turn an option on or off

5 Click **Apply** to see how it looks

6 Repeat for other options until you have it as you want it.

7 Click **OK** to fix the settings and close

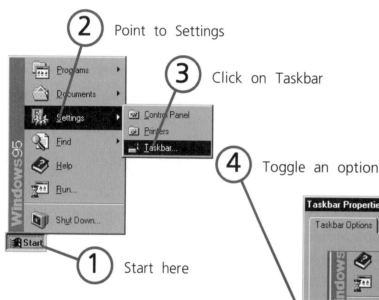

② Point to Settings

③ Click on Taskbar

④ Toggle an option

① Start here

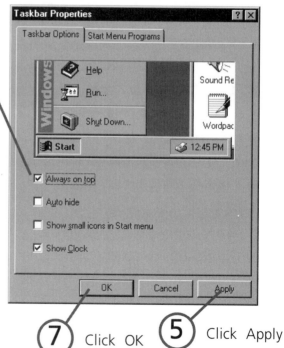

⑦ Click OK   ⑤ Click Apply

Always on Top – when turned off, you can make the Taskbar visible by minimising your applications, or by pressing **[Ctrl]-[Esc]**.

Auto-Hide reduces the Taskbar to a thin line at the bottom of the screen. Pointing at it restores it to size.

Basic steps

Moving

1 Point to any free space on the Taskbar

2 Drag towards the top, left or right of the screen, as desired.

3 Release the mouse button

Resizing

1 Point to the inner edge of the Taskbar

2 When the cursor changes to ↔, drag to change the size of the Taskbar.

Moving and resizing

Moving the Taskbar is quite easy to do by mistake, so it is just as well to know how to do it intentionally – if only to correct a mistake!

Resizing the Taskbar – making it deeper, or wider – is sometimes useful. Narrow vertical displays are almost unreadable.

When you are running a lot of programs with a horizontal Taskbar, the titles on the buttons can be very small. If you deepen the display, you get two rows of decent sized buttons.

Take note

Unless you have a lot of applications running at once, horizontal displays make far better use of screen space.

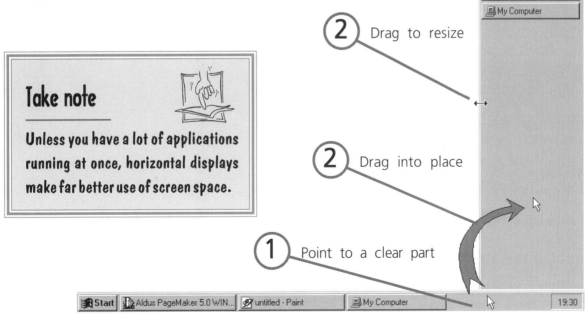

② Drag to resize

② Drag into place

① Point to a clear part

The Start menu

When Windows 95 was installed onto your system, it created a Start menu that included shortcuts to all its own applications and accessories, plus any others that it found on your system. If you had been running Windows 3.1, it will have taken your Program Manager groups and incorporated them into the Start menu structure. When you install new software onto your system, the installation routine should also bring them into the Start menu.

If it gets built automatically, why would we want to mess around with it? The answer is that installation routines can only do so much. They may not structure the menus as you would like. Not all software comes with a routine to install it into Windows 95.

The Start Menu Programs panel of the Taskbar Properties box gives you control of your menu structure.

Use these buttons to change the entries on your menus

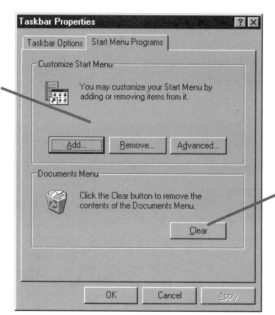

Click here if you ever want to remove all the Documents entries from the Start menu

106

Basic steps

1 Click [Add...]

2 Click [Browse...] and work through your folders to find and select the program

3 Select the menu folder to hold the new entry

4 Replace the program's filename with a more meaningful name

Adding entries

You can add individually any programs that were not handled by the installation routines. All that is essential is that you know where to find them.

Type the path and filename if you like

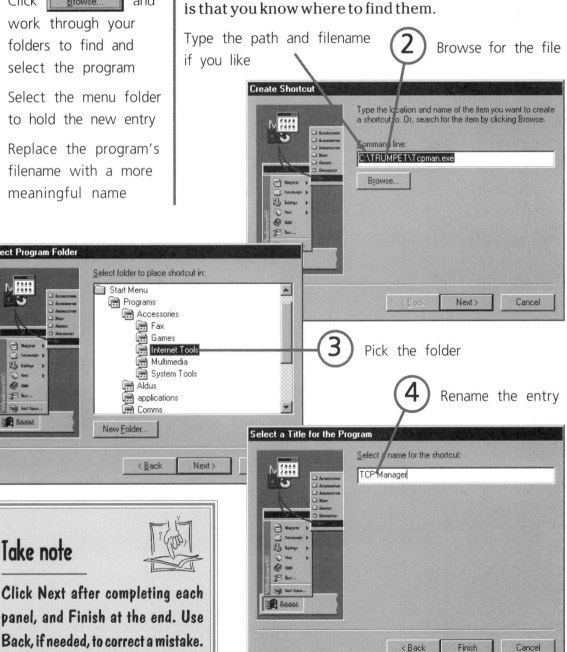

② Browse for the file

③ Pick the folder

④ Rename the entry

Take note

Click Next after completing each panel, and Finish at the end. Use Back, if needed, to correct a mistake.

107

Organising the menu

The Advanced button takes you into Explorer, with the focus on the Start menu folder. From here you can rename, reorganise, delete, create new shortcuts and move them into menu folders. The one job you are most likely to want to do is reorganise.

When you install modern software, you typically get not just one, but several programs – and several menu entries. As well as the application, there will often be a ReadMe First, the Help utility, an uninstall program, and perhaps a clutch of minor utilities. Most of these will be rarely used, and are little more than clutter on the menus.

Unwanted entries can be removed altogether (see page 110), or tucked into their own sub-menu.

(see page 110)

Basic steps

- ❏ Making a sub-menu
1 Click Advanced...
2 Select the over-crowded folder
3 Open the **File** menu and select **New – Folder**
4 Rename the folder
5 Select the excess entries and drag them onto the new folder
6 Close **Explorer**

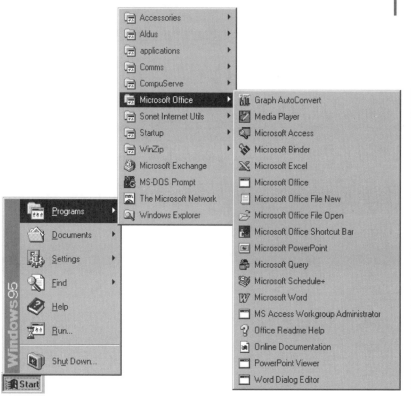

Take note

Office 95 is a classic over-filler of menus. After installation, there are 18 entries in its menu! They are all useful, but some are not wanted often and would be better in a sub-menu.

108

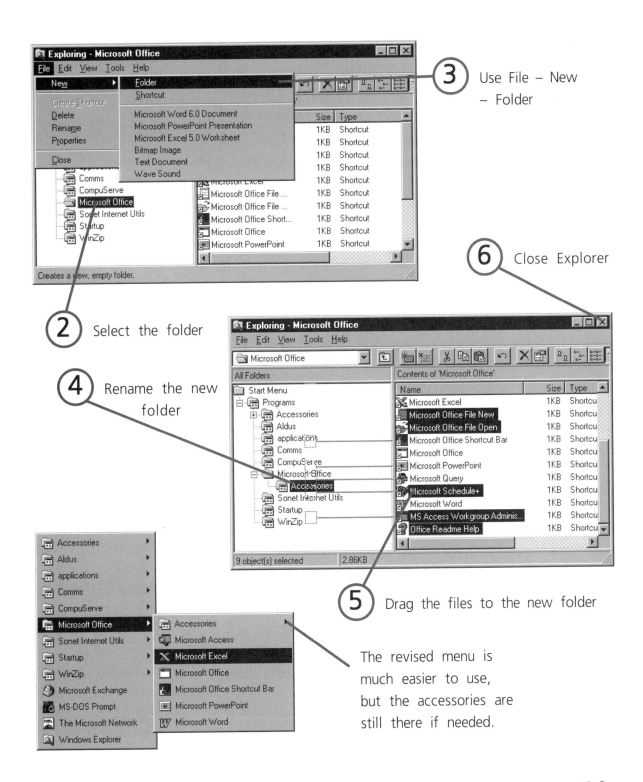

③ Use File – New – Folder

② Select the folder

④ Rename the new folder

⑥ Close Explorer

⑤ Drag the files to the new folder

The revised menu is much easier to use, but the accessories are still there if needed.

109

Removing entries

If you remove software from your system, you will need to remove its entry from the Start menu. You may also want to remove entries for programs that are very rarely used – if necessary they can be added back onto the menu later, or run by double-clicking on tem in Explorer.

Removing entries is even easier than adding new ones. But don't worry about deleting entries by mistake – like all deletions from the hard disk, the entries go first to the Recycle Bin.

Basic steps

1 Click [Remove...]

2 Open up sub-folders if necessary, until you can see the entry.

3 Select the entry

4 Click [Remove...]

5 Repeat steps 2 to 4 as necessary to remove all unwanted entries

6 Click [Close] to return to the Properties panel

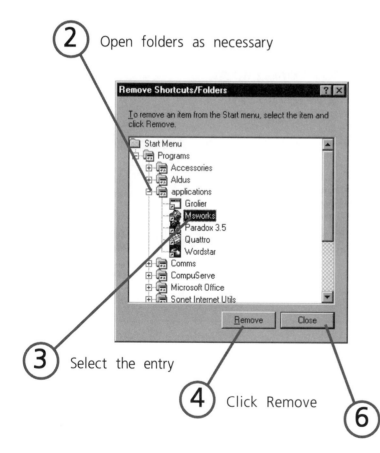

② Open folders as necessary

③ Select the entry

④ Click Remove

⑥ Close when done

Tip

If you send a whole folder to the Recycle Bin by mistake, it will be recreated if you restore one or more of its files.

Basic steps

1 Right click on the clock to open the short menu

2 Select **Adjust Date/Time**

3 Pick the **Month** from the drop down list.

4 Click on the **Day**

5 Click on **Hour, Minute** or **Second** to select then either adjust with the arrows or type the correct value.

6 Click [Apply] to restart the clock.

Setting the Clock

We can't leave the Taskbar without having a look at adjusting the Date and Time. This should not need doing often – PCs keep good time, and Windows 95 even puts the clock forward and back for Summer Time!

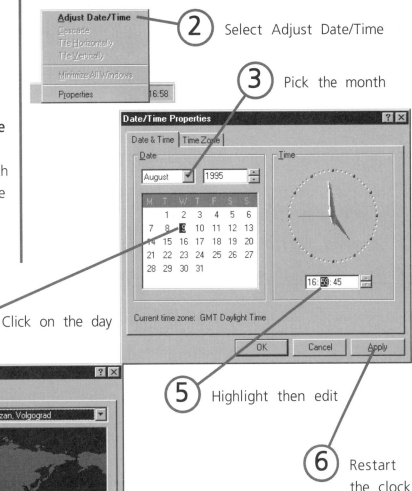

② Select Adjust Date/Time

③ Pick the month

④ Click on the day

⑤ Highlight then edit

⑥ Restart the clock

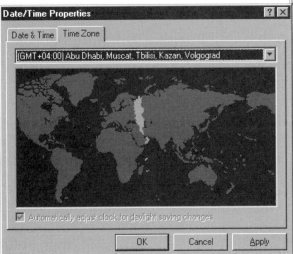

If you want to change the **Time Zone**, either pick the zone from the drop-down list, or click on the zone line and drag it left or right.

Summary

❑ The **Taskbar** can be reduced to a thin line or allowed to lie behind active windows, but is easiest to use if it is visible and always on top.

❑ The Taskbar can be **moved** to any edge of the screen, and **resized** if needed.

❑ The **Start menu** is a folder in the Windows folder. Its entries are folders or shortcuts to programs. It can be managed through Explorer or My Computer, but changes are simpler through the Settings.

❑ You can **add new entries** to the menu by creating shortcuts and storing them in a chosn folder.

❑ The menu can be **reorganised** by moving entries to new or other existing folders.

❑ **Unwanted menu entries** are easily removed.

❑ The **Clock** can be set by opening its short menu.

10 The Control Panel

The settings

The **Control Panel** allows you to customise many of the features of Windows to your own need and tastes.

Some settings are best left at the defaults set by Windows 95; some should be set when new hardware or software is added to the system; some should be set once then left alone; a few can be fiddled with whenever you feel like a change.

Nine of those control settings that can or should be adjusted are covered in this section.

Basic steps

1 Click **Start**

2 Point to **Settings**

3 Select **Control Panel**

Either

4 Right click an icon and **Open** it from the short menu

or

4 Double click on an icon

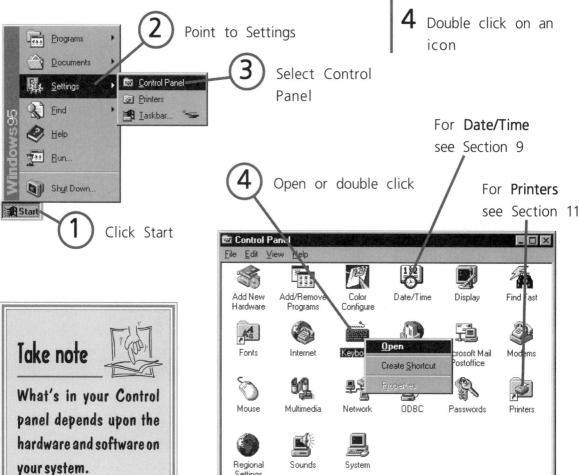

② Point to Settings

③ Select Control Panel

④ Open or double click

① Click Start

For **Date/Time** see Section 9

For **Printers** see Section 11

Take note

What's in your Control panel depends upon the hardware and software on your system.

114

Keyboard

Adjusting the keys

Basic steps

1 Click on the lines beside the pointers to adjust the **Repeat Delay** and **Rate.**

2 Click on the test area and hold down a key.

3 Back to 1 until you are happy.

4 Adjust the **Cursor blink rate** to suit.

5 Click [OK] to fix the settings.

Use the **Language** panel to set up for a second language

This is a small but significant adjustment. When you hold down a key, the system will – after a little while – start to repeat that key's character. This can be very useful if you want a line of dashes or asterisks across the screen.

The two questions are, how long is a little while, and how fast should the characters be repeated?

The answers depend entirely upon your touch. If you are a struggling two-finger typist, go for a Long **Repeat Delay** and a Slow **Repeat Rate** or you will find that you are regularly getting more out of the keyboard than you wanted.

After you have changed a setting, click on the **Test** slot and hold down a key. Do you have easily enough time to get your finger clear before it starts to repeat, and after the system has repeated enough characters?

Only used after fitting a new keyboard

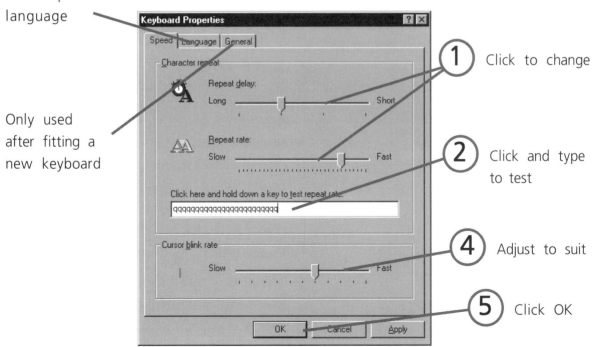

Click to change

Click and type to test

Adjust to suit

Click OK

The Display

Display

This may seem to be pure frills and fancies, but it does have a serious purpose. If you spend a lot of time in front of your screen, being able to see it clearly and use it comfortably is important.

Background panel

The **Wallpaper** is the background to the desktop. Some are hideous, but others are acceptable. The supplied designs can be edited with Paint, if you feel artistic, or you can use any bitmapped graphic of your own. With a large image, set it in the **Centre** rather than duplicate it as a **Tile**.

If you prefer a single colour background, you may want to impose a **Pattern** on it.

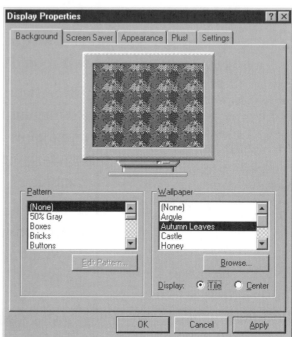

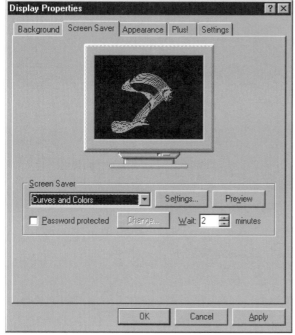

Screen Savers

These are fun but serve little real purpose nowadays. (On an old monitor, if a static image was left on too long, it could burn into the screen.) A screen saver switches to a moving image after the system has been left inactive for a few minutes. **Preview** the ones that are on offer. **Settings** allows you to adjust the images.

There is a small industry churning out weird and wonderful screen savers for you to buy, if you want something different.

Appearance

This controls the colour schemes and the size of fonts. There is a set of ready made schemes, or you can individual parts of the screen from the **Item** list and adjust the **Colour** or **Font**. The scheme can then be saved with a new name.

There are **High Contrast** and coloured **Large** and **Extra large** (font) schemes if easy viewing is needed.

If you make a mess of the scheme – easily done! – restore the appearance by selecting the **Windows Standard**.

Settings

Play with the other panels as much as you like, but treat this one with respect. In particular, do not use **Change Display Type** unless you are unhappy with the current display *and* know what you are doing. You can switch to a display mode that it not properly supported by your hardware, resulting in a screen which is difficult or impossible to read – and therefore to correct!

If you do produce an unreadable screen, reboot the system using the Startup disk – you did make one, didn't you – and restore the default setting from there.

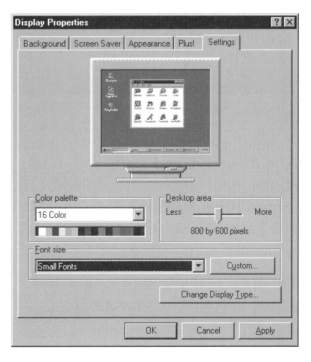

Adjusting the mouse

 Mouse

The **Double-Click Speed** determines the difference between a proper double click and two separate clicks.

Don't change to **Left handed** unless you are the only one who uses the system, and it is the only system that you use. You will only confuse yourself and others.

- ❏ Buttons panel
- 1 Set the **Double click speed**
- 2 Test it
- 3 Click Apply
- ❏ Motion panel
- 4 Set the **Pointer Speed**.
- 5 Test it at the bottom of the panel.
- 6 Click Apply .

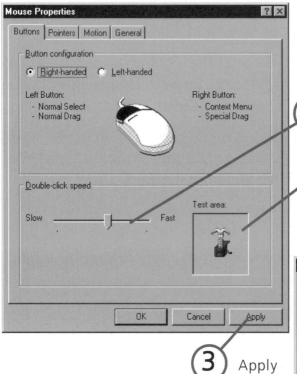

① Adjust

② Test

③ Apply

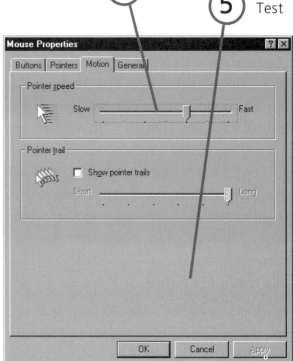

④ Adjust

⑤ Test

The **Pointer Speed** links speed and distance, so that the faster you move the mouse, the further the pointer goes. At the Fastest, a quick flick will take the pointer across the screen.

Pointer Trails make the mouse easier to see on LCD screens of portables.

118

Basic steps

Pointers

- ❏ **Pointers panel**
- **1** Pick a **Scheme**
- **2** Select an action
- **3** Click [Browse...]
- **4** Pick a cursor image for the action
- **5** Click [Open]
- **6** Repeat steps 2 to 5 for any other actions
- **7** Click [OK]

There are alternative Schemes, including ones with large and extra large pointers. You can also pick your own images (and animated ones with Microsoft Plus!) to link to chosen mouse actions.

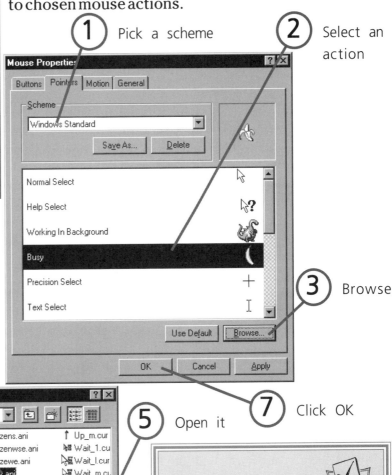

① Pick a scheme

② Select an action

③ Browse

④ Select an image

Check out the Preview

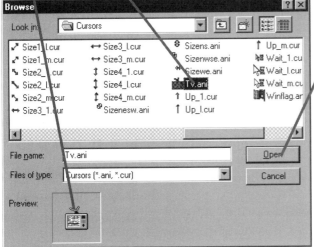

⑤ Open it

⑦ Click OK

Sounds

Sounds

Windows allows you to attach sounds to events. These can be seen as useful ways of alerting you to what's happening or as more modern noise pollution. It all depends upon your point of view. I like a fanfare when the system is ready to start work (to wake me up – well, you wait so long!) and very few other sounds. But try them out – the Utopia sounds are worth listening to.

1 Pick a **Scheme**

2 Select an event.

3 Click ▶ to Preview its sound.

4 Sample a few more.

5 Go back to step 1 and try alternative schemes until you have found the one you like best.

6 To set individual sounds, Browse for an alternative, or select **[none]** for the **Name**.

7 Click Apply or OK

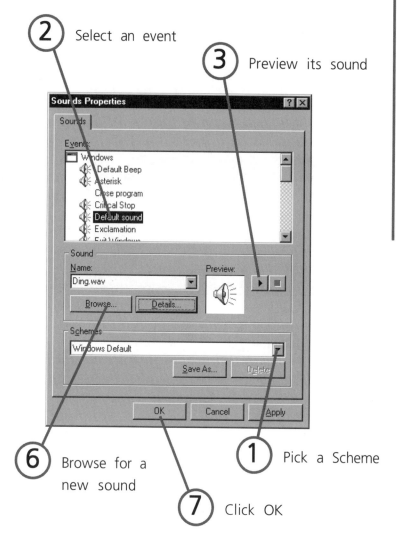

② Select an event

③ Preview its sound

⑥ Browse for a new sound

① Pick a Scheme

⑦ Click OK

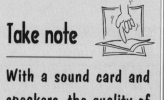

Take note

With a sound card and speakers, the quality of sound compares well to a (cheap) HiFi system. If you are limited to the PC's own speaker, you don't get the same quality, but you can still hear sounds.

Regional Settings

Basic steps

❑ **Date styles**

1 Run **Regional Settings**

2 Open the **Date** panel

3 Pick a **Short date style** from the list and edit it to your taste.

4 Click [Apply]

5 Point to the Taskbar clock and see how it looks.

6 Repeat for the **Long date**.

Regional settings

These control the units of measurement and the styles used by most applications for displaying dates, time, currency and other numbers. The choice of Region in the top panel sets the defaults for the rest.

The other panels are for fine tuning the styles. The **Date** panel is a good example. There are **Short date** and **Long date** styles. Both use the same coding:

Day	Month	
d	M	Number
dd	MM	Number with leading 0 if needed
ddd	MMM	Three letter name
dddd	MMM	Full name
Year	yy for 95; yyyy for 1995	

② Open the Date panel

③ Pick a style and edit

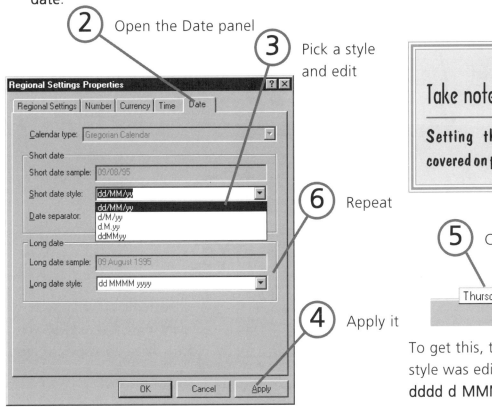

⑥ Repeat

④ Apply it

Take note

Setting the clock is covered on page 111.

⑤ Check it out

To get this, the Long date style was edited to:
dddd d MMMM yyyy

Fonts

Fonts

There is one school of thought that says you can never have enough fonts. There is a decent core supplied with Windows itself, and you will normally acquire more with any word-processor and desktop publishing packages that you install. If these are not enough for you, there are whole disks full of fonts available commercially and through the shareware distributors. Check the adverts in any PC magazine if you are interested.

Installing new fonts is quick and easy.

Basic steps

❑ Adding fonts

1 Place the disk of new fonts into a drive.

2 Open the **File** menu and select **Install New Font**.

3 At the dialog box, select the drive and folder.

4 Wait while the system reads the names of the fonts on the disk.

5 Click [Select All], or work through the list and select the ones you want to install.

6 Click [OK]

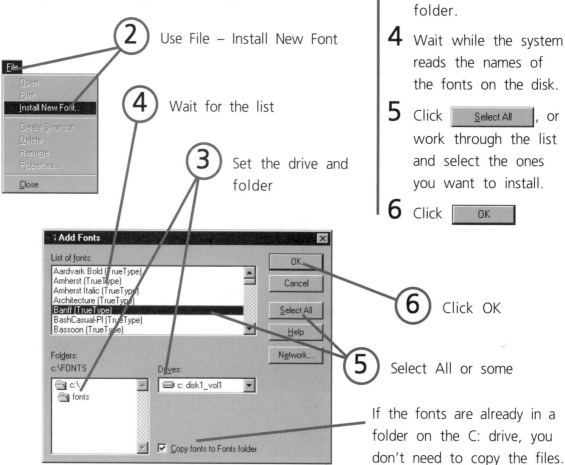

② Use File – Install New Font

④ Wait for the list

③ Set the drive and folder

⑥ Click OK

⑤ Select All or some

If the fonts are already in a folder on the C: drive, you don't need to copy the files.

Basic steps

❏ **Font samples**

1 Select a font.

2 Select **Open** from the **File** menu or the short menu.

3 Click [Print] to see how it looks on paper.

4 Click [Done] to close the viewer.

5 If it is not useful, press **[Delete]** to remove it

Removing unwanted fonts

This is as easy as adding them and well worth doing. You will save space on the hard disk, speed up Windows' start up and have a shorter set to hunt through when you are setting a font in an application.

Open a font file, if you want a detailed sample of the font.

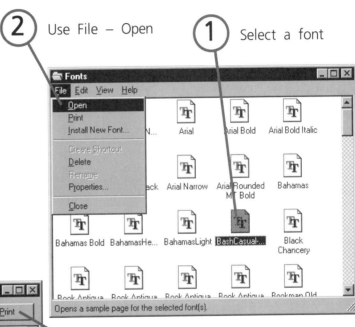

② Use File – Open

① Select a font

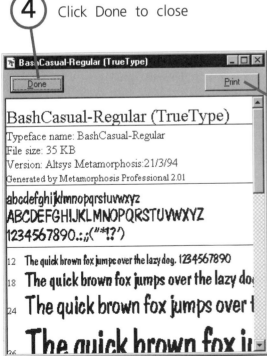

④ Click Done to close

③ Print a sample if wanted

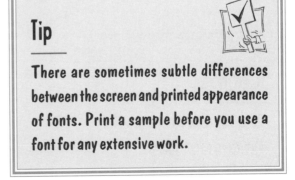

Tip

There are sometimes subtle differences between the screen and printed appearance of fonts. Print a sample before you use a font for any extensive work.

Mail and Fax

Mail and Fax

What options you have here will depend upon whether or not you have a local area network connection or a modem, and whether or not you use have an Internet or other external links.

Most of the properties of all of these will been set during installation, and should not be altered. The main exception is the Fax, where you may want to set your own defaults.

1 Select **Microsoft Fax.**

2 Click **Properties.**

3 Set the transmission **Time**.

4 If your faxes are plain text, they will travel faster if you click **Paper** and select **200 x 100 dpi** resolution

5 Turn on the **Cover page**, if wanted, then select the default.

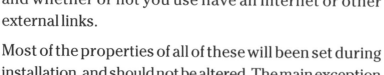

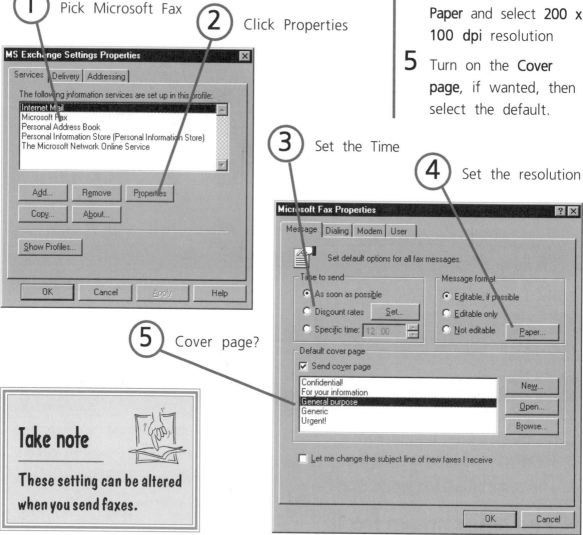

① Pick Microsoft Fax

② Click Properties

③ Set the Time

④ Set the resolution

⑤ Cover page?

Take note

These setting can be altered when you send faxes.

124

Basic steps

System

The System

1 Open the **Performance** panel.

2 Click [File System...].

3 At the **File System Properties** box, open the **CD-ROM** panel.

4 Drop down the list at **Optimize access pattern** and select your type of CD-ROM.

5 Click [OK]

6 [Close] the main box.

Most of the options in this box fall into the look but don't touch category – any changes are best left to the system to handle for itself. There is one exception. You should check that it is optimised for your CD-ROM drive, if you have one.

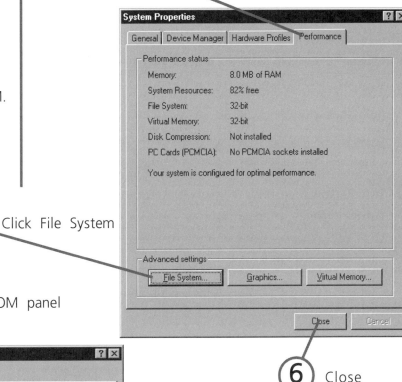

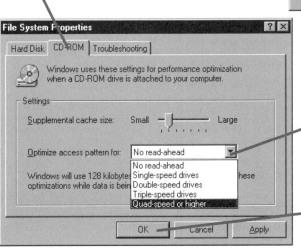

Summary

❑ The **Control Panel** contains routines that determine the settings of some of the most basic features of how Windows works.

❑ Adjust the **mouse** and **keyboard** responses to your own needs at an early stage, then leave them alone.

❑ The **Display** give you plenty of scope for personal preferences. Set the wallpaper, patterns, colour scheme and fonts to suit yourself – but don't change the main settings unless you have to.

❑ There are several **mouse pointer** schemes, and individual pointers can be redesigned.

❑ **Sounds** can be assigned to events, to alert you when things happen.

❑ The **Regional settings** control the appearance of dates, times, currency and numbers in most Windows Applications.

❑ New **Fonts** can be installed easily. It is just as easy to examine fonts and to remove unnecessary ones.

❑ Communications with the outside world are controlled through the **Mail and Fax** settings.

❑ The core **System** settings should be mainly left to the system to manage. It knows what it's doing!

11 Printers

Printer settings

Windows 95 knows about printers, just as it knows about most other bits of hardware that you might attach to your system. If you installed 95 over Windows 3.1, it will have picked up the printer settings from there; if Windows 95 was your first operating system, the printer will have been set up during installation. Either way, as long as you continue to use the same printer, with the same settings, you shouldn't need to bother with the next four pages.

However, things change, and there are alternatives to some of the defaults that are worth exploring.

Basic steps

1 Click **Start**.
2 Point to **Settings**.
3 Select **Printers**.
4 Right click a printer to open its short menu.
5 Select **Properties**.

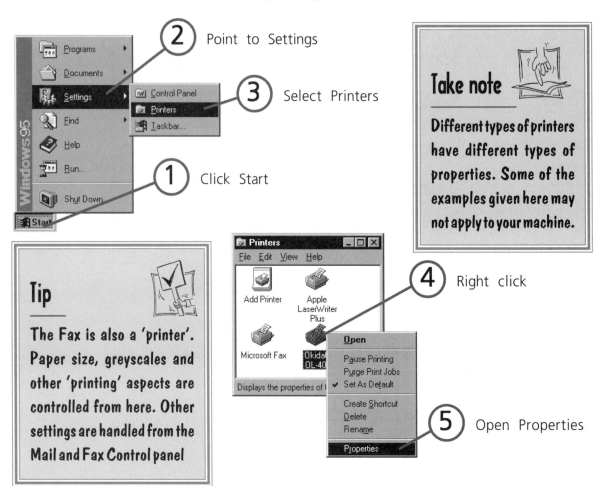

Point to Settings

Select Printers

Click Start

Take note

Different types of printers have different types of properties. Some of the examples given here may not apply to your machine.

Tip

The Fax is also a 'printer'. Paper size, greyscales and other 'printing' aspects are controlled from here. Other settings are handled from the Mail and Fax Control panel

Right click

Open Properties

All printers have a **Paper** panel, with **Paper Size** and **Orientation** options. Alternative **Layouts** are normally only found on Postscript printers

On the **Fonts** panel, if you have the choice, select **Print TrueType as graphics** – this is usually quicker.

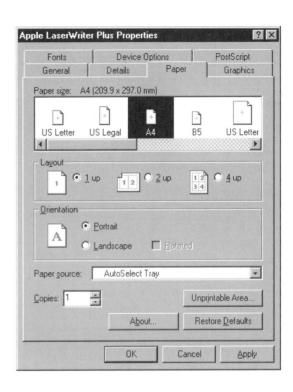

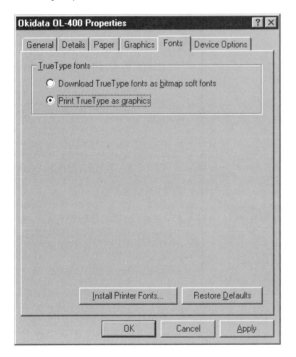

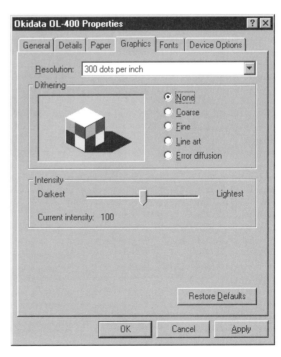

On the **Graphics** panel, you may have **Dithering** options. Dithering can smooth curves and angled lines. Test each option with a page containing a mixture of coloured bitmaps and line drawings to see which gives best results on your printer.

Adding a printer

This is a very easy process, thanks to a helpful little Wizard. Windows 95 has drivers for all the major – and many minor – printers in existence at the time of its design. (Drivers are programs that convert the formatting information from your word-processor or other application into the right codes for the printer.) If you have a *very* new machine, you may need to ask the suppliers for a driver for it.

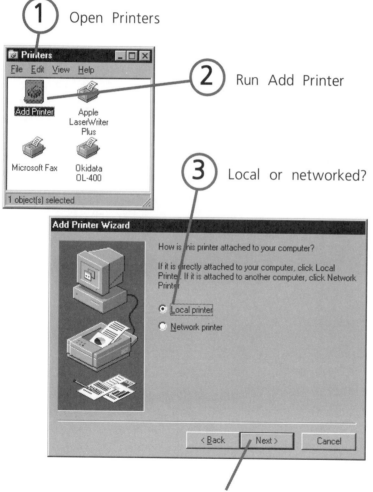

① Open Printers

② Run Add Printer

③ Local or networked?

Click Next at the end of each stage

1 Open the **Printers** folder.

2 Double click **Add Printer.**

3 If you are on a network, select local (attached to your PC) or networked printer.

Either

4 Pick the Manufacturer then the Printer from the lists.

or

5 Insert a disk with the printer driver and click Have Disk.

6 Select the Port – normally LPT1.

7 Change the name if you like – networked printers are often given nicknames to identify them.

8 Set this is the default if appropriate.

9 At the final stage opt for the test print then click FInish and wait.

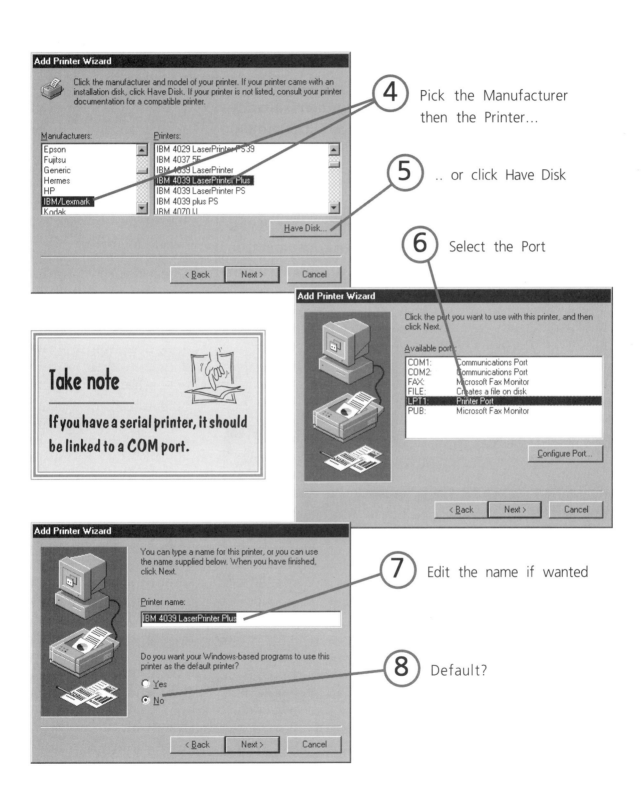

Add Printer Wizard

Click the manufacturer and model of your printer. If your printer came with an installation disk, click Have Disk. If your printer is not listed, consult your printer documentation for a compatible printer.

Manufacturers:

- Epson
- Fujitsu
- Generic
- Hermes
- HP
- IBM/Lexmark
- Kodak

Printers:

- IBM 4029 LaserPrinter PS 39
- IBM 4037 5E
- IBM 4039 LaserPrinter
- IBM 4039 LaserPrinter Plus
- IBM 4039 LaserPrinter PS
- IBM 4039 plus PS
- IBM 4070 IJ

Have Disk...

< Back   Next >   Cancel

④ Pick the Manufacturer then the Printer...

⑤ .. or click Have Disk

⑥ Select the Port

Take note

If you have a serial printer, it should be linked to a COM port.

Add Printer Wizard

Click the port you want to use with this printer, and then click Next.

Available ports:

COM1:	Communications Port
COM2:	Communications Port
FAX:	Microsoft Fax Monitor
FILE:	Creates a file on disk
LPT1:	Printer Port
PUB:	Microsoft Fax Monitor

Configure Port...

< Back   Next >   Cancel

Add Printer Wizard

You can type a name for this printer, or you can use the name supplied below. When you have finished, click Next.

Printer name:

IBM 4039 LaserPrinter Plus

Do you want your Windows-based programs to use this printer as the default printer?

○ Yes
● No

< Back   Next >   Cancel

⑦ Edit the name if wanted

⑧ Default?

Managing the queue

When you send a document for printing, Windows 95 will happily handle it in the background. It prepares the file for the printer, stores it in a queue if the printer is already busy or off-line, pushes the pages out one at a time and deletes the temporary files it has created. Nothing visible happens on screen – unless the printer runs out of paper or has other faults.

This is fine when things run smoothly. However, if you decide you want to cancel the printing of a document, or have sent several and want to push one to the head of the queue, then you do need to see things. No problem!

Basic steps

1 Open the **Printers** folder.

2 Right click the active printer and select **Open** from its menu.

❑ **To change the order**

3 Select the file you want to move.

4 Drag it up or down to its new position.

❑ **To cancel printing**

5 Select the file(s).

6 Press **[Delete]** or open the **Document** menu and select **Cancel Printing**.

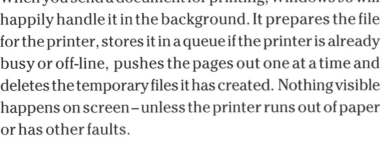

① Open Printers

Open the active printer's panel ②

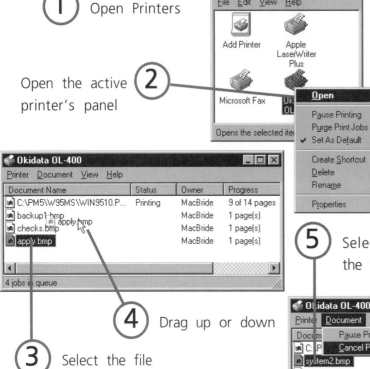

④ Drag up or down

③ Select the file

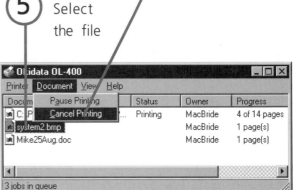

⑤ Select the file

⑥ Cancel Printing

Basic steps

1 Open the **Printers** folder

2 Open the folder containing the document file to be printed.

3 Arrange the windows so that you can see both clearly.

4 Drag the file across and drop it on the printer icon.

Direct printing

You do not necessarily have to load a document into an application to print it. Windows 95 can print many types of documents directly from the files. Bitmapped graphics (.BMP files), plain text and the documents from any Microsoft Office application can be printed in this way, as can those from other newer software.

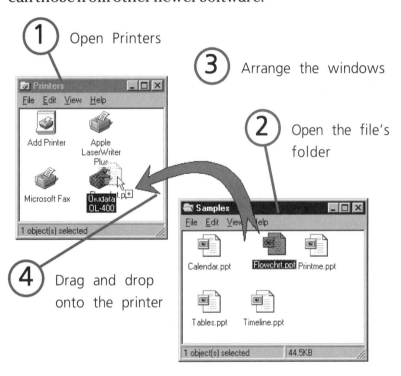

① Open Printers

③ Arrange the windows

② Open the file's folder

④ Drag and drop onto the printer

Tip

Combine this technique with Quick View, so that you make sure you print the right thing. It makes for a quick and easy way to output existing files.

Take note

You can use this method to print on machines that are not connected to your PC. Simply store the document file on floppy and drag it onto the printer icon on the PC attached to the printer you want to use.

133

Summary

❑ Printer settings can be adjusted if wanted. The **Paper**, **Graphics** and **Font** options should be checked.

❑ **Adding a new printer** is easy, thanks to the Wizard. Windows 95 is equipped with drivers for almost all printers currently in use, though you may need a manufacturer's disk with very new models.

❑ Printing is handled in the **background**, so that – apart from slowing things up a bit – it does not interfere with your other work.

❑ Files are stored in a **queue** before printing. You can change their order or delete them if necessary.

❑ You can **print** a document **directly**, rather than through its application, by dragging the file to the printer icon.

12 Useful tools

The Clipboard

The Clipboard is a mechanism for copying and moving text, graphics, files, folders and other types of data within and between applications. Whatever you are doing in Windows, it is always at hand and used in the same way.

Any Windows application that handles data in any form has an Edit menu. This always contains three core options – Cut, Copy and Paste – plus varying others. You can see these on the two Edit menus shown below.

- **Cut** removes a selected block of text or object, and transfers it to the Clipboard's memory.

- **Copy** takes a copy of the selected item into the Clipboard, but without removing it.

- **Paste** copies whatever is in the Clipboard into the current cursor position in the application.

❑ **To Cut**

1 Select the text or object.

2 Open the **Edit** menu.

3 Click **Cut**.

❑ **To Copy**

1 Select the text or object.

2 Open the **Edit** menu.

3 Click **Copy**.

❑ **To Paste from the Clipboard**

1 Place the cursor at the point where you want the selected item to be inserted.

2 Open the **Edit** menu.

3 Click **Paste**.

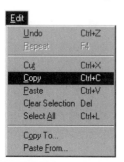

The Edit menus from Paint (left) and WordPad (below). The core options are always there.

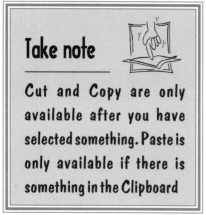

Take note

Cut and Copy are only available after you have selected something. Paste is only available if there is something in the Clipboard

Tip

See page 67 for copying files and folders through the Clipboard.

Basic steps

Selecting for Cut and Copy

❑ **To select text**

1 Place the text cursor at the start of the block.

2 Drag the pointer to spread a highlight over the block.

3 You are ready to Cut or Copy.

❑ **To select one object**

1 Click on it to get handles around its edges.

❑ **To select a set of adjacent objects**

1 Imagine a rectangle that will enclose all the objects.

2 Place the pointer at one corner of this rectangle.

3 Drag the broken outline to enclose them all.

4 Release the mouse button and check that all have acquired handles.

These techniques should work with most Windows application. Some will also offer additional selection methods of their own, which may be more convenient in some situations.

You normally select **text** by dragging the pointer over the desired block of characters.

The highlight shows the selected text.

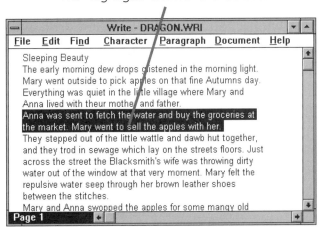

With DTP, or other applications that work with **objects** – including the cells of spreadsheets and tables – you select a single object by clicking on it, or a group of objects by dragging an outline around them all.

The enclosing outline

Selected objects are usually indicated by handles.

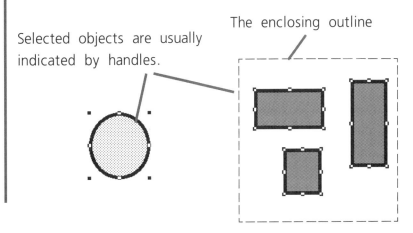

Copying the screen

When a PC is in MS-DOS mode, pressing **[Print Screen]** will send a copy of the screen directly to the printer. When you are working in Windows, the copy goes to the Clipboard. This gives you the chance to edit it before printing, or to pass it on to an application.

● **[Print Screen]** copies the entire screen.

● **[Alt]-[Print Screen]** copies the active window.

The screen snapshot can then be pasted directly into a suitable application – a graphics or DTP package, or a word-processor that can handle graphics. If you want to edit it first, paste it into Paint. The screen samples in this book were all produced by capturing the screen or window, and editing as necessary in Paint.

Basic steps

❑ **Copying the screen**

1 Tidy up the screen, removing or minimising unwanted windows, and arranging the others to focus your message clearly.

2 Press **[Print Screen]**.

3 Move to the application into which you want to insert the snapshot, or to Paint.

4 Open the **Edit** menu and **Paste**.

❑ **Copying a window**

1 Adjust the size of the window to fit text or image you want to display.

2 Hold **[Alt]** and press **[Print Screen]**.

3 **Paste** the snapshot into the target application.

Character Map

The Character map

Basic steps

1 Go to the **Accessories** menu and select **Character Map**.

2 Select the **Font**.

3 Click on a character to highlight it.

4 Click [Select] to place it into **Characters to Copy**.

5 Go back over 3 and 4 as necessary.

6 Click [Copy] to copy to the Clipboard.

7 Return to your application and **Paste** the characters into it.

This shows the full set of characters that are present in any given font, and allows you to select one or more individual characters for copying into other applications. Its main use is probably for picking up Wingdings for decoration, or the odd foreign letter or mathematical symbols in otherwise straight text.

The characters are rather small, but you can get a better look at a character, by holding the mouse button down while you point at it. This produces an enlarged image.

(2) Select the Font

(3) Highlight a character

(6) Click Copy

(4) Click Select

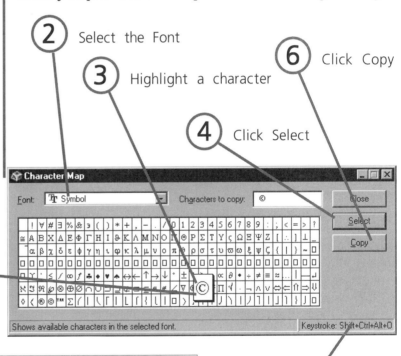

Hold down the button to magnify

Note the keystroke

Tip

If you are going to use a character often, learn its keystroke. This is shown at the bottom right. For Alt+ ones, hold [Alt] and type the number on the Number Pad.

139

The Phone Dialer

I find this very useful. It gives one-touch dialling – more reliably than the speed dial on my phone, which has the memory of a goldfish. Phone dial does not forget, and entering and editing numbers is easy.

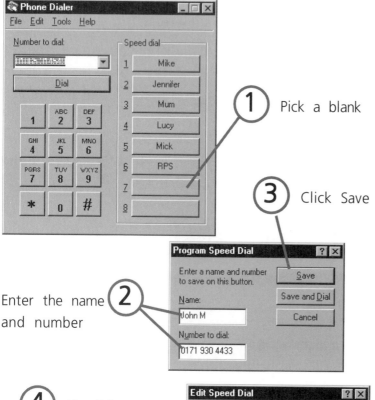

Pick a blank ①

Click Save ③

Enter the name and number ②

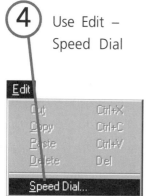

Use Edit – Speed Dial ④

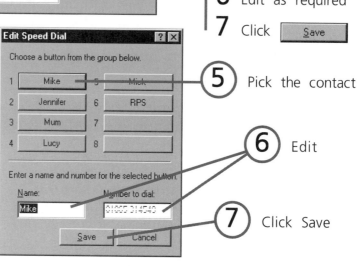

Pick the contact ⑤

Edit ⑥

Click Save ⑦

Basic steps

To find **Phone Dialer**, click **Start** point to **Programs** then **Accessories**

❏ **Entering a number**

1 Click on a blank button.

2 Enter the name and number in the **Speed Dial** panel

3 Click   Save

❏ **Editing a number**

4 Open the **Edit** menu and select **Speed Dial**

5 Click on the contact to change.

6 Edit as required

7 Click   Save

Basic steps

❑ Dialing

Either

1 Select a contact

or

1 Enter a number directly on the keypad

2 Pick up the phone

3 Click [Dial]

4 Wait for it to dial the number and give a high pitched tone, then click [Talk]

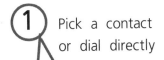

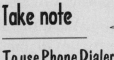
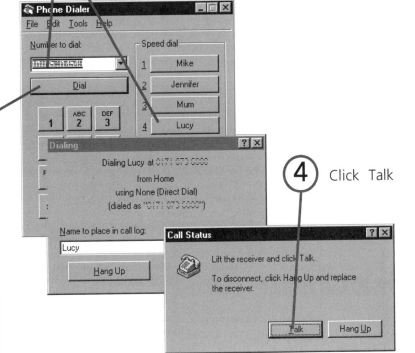

① Pick a contact or dial directly

③ Click Dial

④ Click Talk

141

MS-DOS programs

Some DOS programs can be run directly from within Windows 95, simply by adding them to the Start menu. Set them to run in a Window, rather than Full Screen, to gives you access to the Edit facilities. The number of screen lines and the font can be adjusted to suit yourself.

Basic steps

❏ Setting up

1 Open the **Properties** dialog box for the program's shortcut.

2 Switch to the **Screen** panel.

3 Check that the **Usage** is set to **Window**.

4 Set the **Initial size**.

Open the Screen panel

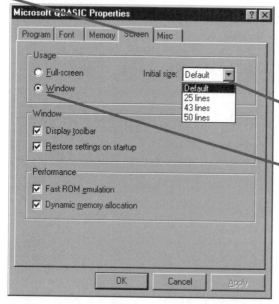

Set the Size

Run in a window

Turn on the Toolbar in DOS windows for easy editing and font control.

The MS-DOS Prompt

This gives you the standard DOS C:> prompt. Use it for those programs that will not run from a shortcut, or that are raely used.

Make sure the MS-DOS Prompt is set to run in a window.

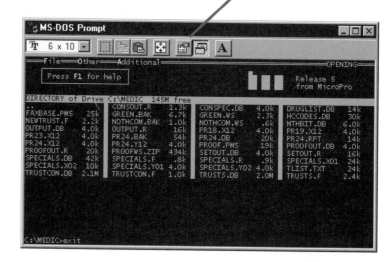

Basic steps

☐ Copying

1 Open the **Control** menu.

2 Select **Edit**, then **Mark**.

3 Highlight the text you want to copy.

4 Open the Control menu again and select **Edit – Copy**.

5 Switch to your target application and paste the text there.

Copy and Paste in MS-DOS

There is an Edit item in the Control menu in DOS windows, and a set of Toolbar icons that can be used to copy text between DOS and Windows applications. Pasting is the same as normal, but to copy you must first use **Edit – Mark** to highlight the block of text. To do this, imagine a rectangle that encloses the text. Point to one corner and drag the highlight to the opposite corner.

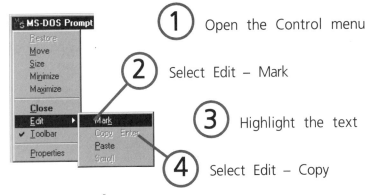

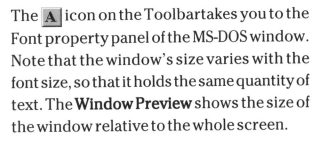

① Open the Control menu

② Select Edit – Mark

③ Highlight the text

④ Select Edit – Copy

Fonts

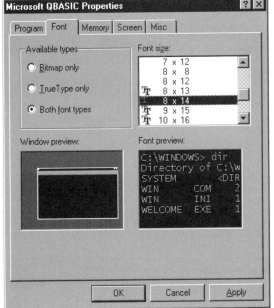

The **A** icon on the Toolbar takes you to the Font property panel of the MS-DOS window. Note that the window's size varies with the font size, so that it holds the same quantity of text. The **Window Preview** shows the size of the window relative to the whole screen.

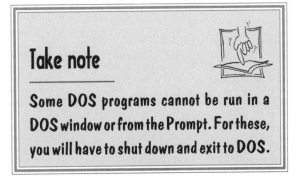

Take note

Some DOS programs cannot be run in a DOS window or from the Prompt. For these, you will have to shut down and exit to DOS.

Summary

❑ The **Clipboard** is used for copying text and graphics within and between programs, and for copying files and folders across disks and folders.

❑ **Text can be selected** by dragging a highlight over it.

❑ Individual **images and files can be selected** by clicking on them. Groups of objects can be selected by dragging outlines around them.

❑ An image of the screen can be captured by pressing **[Print Screen]**. An image of the current window can be captured by pressing **[Alt]–[Print Screen]**.

❑ The **Character map** allows you to select special characters from a selected font, to paste into an application.

❑ If your phone is connected through your modem/PC system, you can use the **Phone Dialer** for quick and easy dialling.

❑ **MS-DOS programs** can be run directly from shortcuts, or through the MS-DOS prompt. In either case, they should be set to run in a window, not full screen, to get access to the cut and paste facilities.

144

Microsoft Plus!

Microsoft Plus! is a package of add-ons to Windows 95, aimed mainly at those users with more powerful systems. It is a mixture of utilities and fripperies.

DriveSpace3 is an advanced disk compressor, and useful if you have a hard drive larger than 250Mb. (See page 99.)

System Agent allows you to set up routines to perform housekeeping chores at scheduled times or when the PC is idle. This is probably most useful on networked machines, or those with multiple users.

The **Internet Jumpstart Kit** will give you what you need to connect to the Internet. Useful if you do not already have a connection, but note that Internet access via Microsoft will not be available in the UK until mid-1996.

Desktop themes are covered on the next page.

Dial Up Networking Server is for those that want to let other remote users link into their system.

Take note

As with other parts of Windows 95, you can select components either at installation or later, using the Add/Remove Programs item in the Control Panel.

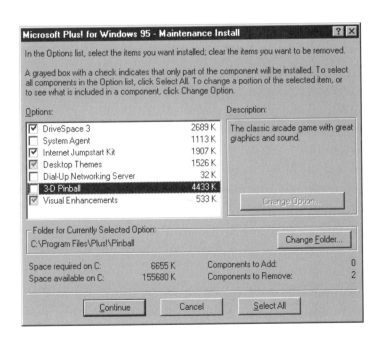

3-D Pinball is a game. Cool graphics and slick action – as long as you like pinball.

The **Visual Enhancements** include better representation of fonts, animated pointers and a routine to stretch a Wallpaper image to fill the screen. For these, your screen must handle at least 256 colours; some need more than that.

A **Desktop theme** links wallpaper, icons, pointers, sounds and other parts of the desktop around a common concept. They are cleverly done but purely decorative. Some will work on 256-colour screens; others require higher colour resolution. *Dangerous Creatures*, right, has hilarious icons and pointers.

Microsoft Plus! adds another panel to the Display Properties to handle the visual enhancements and themed icons. Note that the **Stretch Wallpaper to fill screen** option does precisely that – if the graphic that you are using as a wallpaper is not the same proportions as the screen, it will be distorted.

146

Index